D1498953

HUNGRY *for* LOUISIANA

HUNGRY *for* LOUISIANA

AN OMNIVORE'S JOURNEY

MAGGIE HEYN RICHARDSON

ILLUSTRATIONS BY ELIZABETH RANDALL NEELY

LOUISIANA STATE UNIVERSITY PRESS

BATON ROUGE

Published with the assistance of the Borne Fund

Published by Louisiana State University Press
Copyright © 2015 by Louisiana State University Press
Manufactured in the United States of America
FIRST PRINTING

DESIGNER: Mandy McDonald Scallan
TYPEFACE: Whtiman
PRINTER AND BINDER: Maple Press, Inc.

Library of Congress Cataloging-in-Publication Data

Richardson, Maggie Heyn, 1969–
 Hungry for Louisiana : an Omnivore's journey / Maggie Heyn
Richardson ; illustrations by Elizabeth Randall Neely.
  pages cm
 ISBN 978-0-8071-5835-7 (cloth : alk. paper) — ISBN 978-0-
8071-5836-4 (pdf) — ISBN 978-0-8071-5837-1 (epub) — ISBN)
978-0-8071-5838-8 (mobi) 1. Cooking, American—Louisiana
style. 2. Food industry and trade—Louisiana. 3. Food habits—
Louisiana. I. Title.
 TX715.2.L68R53 2015
 641.59763—dc23

2014047033

FOR JOHN

CONTENTS

ACKNOWLEDGMENTS

First, sincere thanks goes to the many friends, acquaintances, and strangers in this magical, peculiar place who filled my head with story ideas over the more than two decades I have lived here, even if they didn't realize it.

I am deeply grateful to my editor at the Louisiana State University Press, Alisa Plant, for her ability to extract workable ideas around our mutual joy, Louisiana food, and to ease my neuroses and make the book-writing process so enjoyable. Thanks to Poppy Tooker for superb content suggestions and for Creole cream cheese details. I am also in John T. Edge's debt for his support and encouragement in the project's first stages. The Southern Foodways Alliance at the University of Mississippi provided excellent oral history on Louisiana food producers. Historian and author Sara Roahen's work on boudin was especially helpful, as were Cynthia Lejeune Nobles's chapters in *New Orleans Cuisine: Fourteen Signature Dishes and Their Histories* and James Q. Salter's *Zwolle, Louisiana; Our Story.*

Thanks to scholars Wayne Parent and Ryan Orgera for inviting me to write the food chapter in their book *The Louisiana Field Guide* (LSU Press, 2014), a process that helped shape this project. Thanks to Wayne and to former LSU College of Humanities and Social Sciences dean Gaines Foster for making me part of their class on southern identity at LSU.

Research for this project relied on busy people sharing their time and expertise with me. Heartfelt thanks go to Sam Irwin, Elizabeth Hill, Cheramie Sonnier, Aaron Melancon, Ray McClain, Dean Wilson, Jody Meche, Bill Pizzolato, Hal Bailey, Louis Marien, Carl Verzwyvelt, Jody

Elisar, Jackie Loewer, Steve Linscombe, Celeste Dolan, Robbie Trahan, Scott Duplechein, Isaac Toups, Angela Vercher, Edward Braud III, Audrey Braud, Katie Mauthe Cutrer, Kenny Mauthe, Jamie Mauthe, John Folse, Ashley Hansen, Don Elbers, Ronnie Sciortino, Victoria Moseley Bayless, Donna Black, Claude Black, Lionel Key, Earl Gaudet, Jack Losso, Dudley Passman, Lester Bourgeois, Donald Bourgeois, Beau Bourgeois, Calvin Hue, Chris Derocher, Bob Carriker, Jim Jenkins, Larry Babineaux, Rodney Babineaux, Ginger Box, Bernie Box, Kathleen E. R. Smith, Judy Garcia, Ethel Diener, Rebecca Loupe, Quinn Bowermeister, Lee Anne Garner, Jason Gilfour, Jarod Voisin, Patrick Banks, and the late Mike Voisin.

Sara Bongiorni and Blake Newton took time to read and edit chapters. Sara Murphy and Betty Schroeder enthusiastically tested recipes. Belle Blanchard Newton spent countless hours over several months providing invaluable comments on the entire manuscript. Stafford Wood, Kate Metcalf, and Mary Kneeland Metcalf provided helpful insight into the book's marketing. Thank you.

I am grateful to my Blanchard aunts, uncles, and cousins for their consistent loyalty and support. Thanks to my father and stepmother, Christopher and Gail Heyn, for their love and for fostering my lifelong appreciation for a well-told story. Before, during, and after the project, my mother-in-law, Helen Richardson, was always ready to babysit and share her good cheer. Thanks to my late stepfather, Jerry Smith, for ceaseless grace and optimism. And I'm forever in debt to my mother, Peggy Blanchard Smith, who still teaches me writing's most important lesson, to listen.

Finally, thanks to my children, Marien, Christopher, and Mercer Richardson, fonts of entertainment, affection, and inspiration, and to my husband, John Richardson, who understands big dreams and embodies generosity. I can never repay the four of them for diffusing my shortcomings with their patience and devotion and for making life one delicious ride.

HUNGRY *for* LOUISIANA

INTRODUCTION

Bayou State of Mind

I fell headlong into Louisiana's seductive food culture after moving to the state in the early nineties to attend graduate school at Louisiana State University (LSU) in Baton Rouge. Growing up in Georgia, I was raised with a deep appreciation for the signature foods of my corner of the world: fried chicken, boiled peanuts, peach cobbler, and pork-centric pit barbecue—foods that also happened to be claimed by other parts of the southern United States. Louisiana's culinary texture, I quickly learned, was markedly different. At every turn, I found unusual flavors and preparation methods that had little in common with the rest of the South. But even more noticeable was food's heightened social significance. As it does across the globe, the traditions of the table cemented the bond between family and friends—but in the Bayou State, food was also the clockwork that set life to an insistent rhythm.

I first arrived in Baton Rouge in the spring, when crawfish season was well underway, and it didn't take long to see how this annual event established a shared recreational pattern. As newcomers do, I scored numerous invitations to crawfish boils where friends and acquaintances gathered around newspaper-covered tables piled with scarlet "mudbugs" poured from giant aluminum pots. There always seemed to be a crawfish boil happening somewhere, giving a greenhorn like me ample opportunity to master the art of extracting tail meat from the small crustacean's shell. I adored its sweet-spicy flavor and tender texture, and the sensation of a cold beer chaser. But what I loved more was the comfort of being locked in a common purpose with others who, regardless of life's pressing demands, were taking time to laugh, listen, and savor the seasonal bounty.

Crawfish boils only scratched the surface of Louisiana's food rituals. On Mondays, red beans and rice pervaded restaurant menus throughout the state—a New Orleans custom stemming from washday Mondays, when working women needed a one-pot meal that simmered unattended. Fall meant heading to LSU's Tiger Stadium for communal meals served by friendly, passionate fans. And every sixth of January, on the Feast of the Epiphany, rectangular boxes holding the first of the season's Mardi Gras king cakes emerged in grocery stores and bakeries. For the next several weeks until Ash Wednesday, I, and everyone I knew, scooped up these cinnamon-strewn pastry rings iced in shades of purple, green, and gold and brought them home, to school, or to the office. The lucky person served the slice with the plastic baby Jesus tucked inside was responsible for bringing the next king cake—a practice that says more about the need for sustained celebrations here than it does about piety.

As the months, and years, went on, I eased further into Louisiana's relaxed pace and met plenty of other transplants who were also marveling at the state's homey, exotic food culture. When we weren't sharing a meal, we were discussing our latest culinary finds, from road food gems to seafood boil formulas. The unassuming and welcoming manner of Louisianans was startling. They felt a kind of Old World pride for their food traditions, but they didn't secret them away; they shared them eagerly. I found myself striking up conversations with perfect strangers about food—and my questions were almost always satisfied with generous, eager responses.

Graduate school ended, but by then, the Louisiana lifestyle had set its hook. The state had its share of well-documented social and financial woes, landing at the bottom of national rankings in literacy, health care, and other issues. But I couldn't resist. The people had enveloped me in their warmth, and the culture was relentlessly appealing. I remained in the state, eventually embarking on a career as a freelance journalist, marrying a native, and starting a family.

Food occupies a significant part of the collective consciousness of Louisianans as well as anyone like me who has lived in the state long enough to absorb its compelling customs. We can talk endlessly about food, debating questions that have the power to forge a momentary bond between two people who might not have anything else in common: *Who has the flakiest po'boy? Where'd you get your boudin? Did you try that new restaurant in New Orleans? Have you made friends with that farmers market vendor?* We devote considerable energy to planning gatherings with friends and family—boiling crawfish, shrimp, and crab, frying fresh catfish, smoking whole pigs in contraptions called Cajun Microwaves, and making bread pudding from stale baguettes and pantry staples—with the sole intention of feeding whoever shows up.

By the time Louisiana children have reached adulthood, they have absorbed a strong sense of their state's culinary philosophy and some have learned how to prepare many of its emblematic dishes. If they move away as adults, they feel Louisiana's gravitational pull, lamenting the absence of its food traditions and seeking out other Bayou State natives with whom to pine for the flavors of home. All over the United States, groups of expatriates have established recurring social events— some called Louisiana Drinking Clubs—where they might share a care package of pork cracklins, hog's head cheese, or Community Coffee, a century-old brand founded and based in Baton Rouge. One of LSU's most reliable methods of fundraising is to organize crawfish boils in cities where large groups of alumni live, because acting out the springtime ceremony strikes an emotional chord. It fills that powerful human need to associate with something larger than oneself—to be part of something vibrant and meaningful.

More of today's food lovers are wary of industrial farming and mass production, and they prioritize foods that are grown and produced in close proximity to where they're sold. Consequently, farmers markets have been flourishing across the country, and a growing number of restaurants are trumpeting the local provenance of menu items. Even if a consumer doesn't participate in this new trend, he is certainly aware of the local foods movement and the value assigned to fruits, vegetables, meat, dairy, and other goods produced and enjoyed within a tight radius.

In Louisiana, celebrating the regional bounty never fully faded in the first place. While the state has embraced its share of big box stores and fast food and chain restaurants, there remains a powerful attachment to small family purveyors and to ingredients that spring from local waterways, farms, and fields. Local and seasonal aren't fleeting culinary trends here. They are embedded deep in the psyche and have always been part of the shared routine.

Spring signals the arrival of not just crawfish but native strawberries and vast amounts of produce that most of the rest of the country won't see until summer. It's also the start of *hundreds* of food festivals that celebrate the state's culinary riches, from jambalaya to *cochon de lait* (suckling pig). Spring also marks the beginning of shrimp season, when rubber-boot-clad shrimpers speed into coastal waters to net brown shrimp. White shrimp follow later in the season. Summer brings blue crabs and endless figs, blueberries, peaches, watermelon, tomatoes, and the return of "snoball" stands that sell fine, shaved ice drenched in sweet syrup. Fall is dominated by football tailgate parties, where die-hard fans establish what could pass for tent cities around LSU's Tiger Stadium and other arenas. Often starting preparation the evening before the game, tailgaters turn out elaborate Cajun and Creole menus using souped-up outdoor cooking equipment. Winter brings gumbo in its many variations, plump oysters from Gulf estuaries, shrimp-stuffed *mirlitons* (chayotes) on holiday tables, and oranges, grapefruits, kumquats, and satsumas from backyards and citrus groves, especially in the parishes south of New Orleans.

Louisiana's foodways aren't accidental. They have evolved over more than three hundred years in the state's cities and on its farms, thanks to a vibrant mix of cultures and abundant raw materials. Thrifty immigrants arriving in the territory in the late seventeenth century stumbled upon waters rife with edible creatures, lush woods that harbored game, and promising farming conditions. They fused their ancestral food traditions with newfound ingredients, many unfamiliar, producing new dishes that would form the basis of *Creole* cuisine in the word's original sense—a unique blend of the Old and New Worlds.

The French were the first Europeans to claim the Louisiana territory, after René-Robert Cavalier, Sieur de La Salle, traversed the Mississippi River beginning in 1682 and asserted that the lands drained by the Mississippi now belonged to France. After the French made New Orleans the colony's capital in 1722, scores of French settlers established themselves in and around the port city and settled into a new life. They integrated New World ingredients into their cooking methods, finding familiar items along the way, including oysters and crayfish (crawfish). The colonists discovered that European crops such as wheat failed to thrive in the humid, subtropical climate, so they learned to grow corn with help from local Native Americans. It was hard at first, but eventually, the territory's year-round growing season and availability of wild game and livestock sustained—and inspired—its new residents.

Slaves from West Africa and from the French colonies of the Caribbean were brought to the Louisiana colony during the same period. They introduced an awareness of rice, okra, and stews and were the likely architects of gumbo. Germans also arrived in the early eighteenth century, settling around New Orleans in present-day St. Charles and St. James parishes (still known today as the German Coast), where they set up successful dairy farms and sausage-making operations. In the late nineteenth century, additional waves of German immigrants who settled in the Acadiana region of the state would help establish Louisiana's rice industry.

Spain claimed much of the Louisiana territory after 1763, a consequence of the Peace of Paris after the Seven Years' War in Europe when France, Great Britain, and Spain shuffled many of their North American holdings. Spanish settlers carried their gastronomic traditions to the Louisiana territory, including paella, the one-pot Valencian rice dish made with seafood, saffron, and sausage. It formed the basis of jambalaya. Spanish settlers in adjacent New Spain (present-day Mexico) also brought the tamale and empanada (meat pie) to Louisiana when they established permanent residences after their military service in the northwest region of the state. The pork tamale would become the signature food of the town of Zwolle, while the city of Natchitoches would build its identity around meat pies.

During the Spanish period, one of Louisiana's most significant immigrant groups arrived—the Acadians. Living in the Canadian province of Nova Scotia, then known as Acadia, these tight-knit Catholic descendants of French peasants refused to take an oath to Great Britain's Protestant king George II. Consequently, they were expelled from the province by the British and relocated to various colonies in the Atlantic and Caribbean, eventually making their way to south Louisiana. The Acadians brought their frugal cooking traditions and farming and trapping acumen to the Atchafalaya River Basin, to the prairie west of Lafayette, and to the bayous south of New Orleans. Their efficient use of local crops and livestock (especially the pig) inspired the birth of the well-seasoned Everyman fare that became known as Cajun cuisine.

Meanwhile, in 1777, the Spanish government ordered about seven hundred Canary Islanders, many poor tenant farmers, to Louisiana to help increase the colony's population. These transplants eventually settled in St. Bernard and Plaquemines parishes, bringing an understanding of cattle ranching and sugar-cane farming, the latter becoming one of the most significant agricultural industries in the state. Louisiana is the second largest producer of sugar cane today, behind only Florida. The descendants of the Canary Islanders, the Isleños, still celebrate their culture and traditions with an annual festival in St. Bernard Parish.

In 1803, President Thomas Jefferson completed the purchase of the Louisiana territory from France, and in 1812, Louisiana was admitted to the union as the eighteenth state. Throughout the nineteenth century, the state's food culture continued to adapt and sharpen. By midcentury, Croatian fishermen had settled in Plaquemines Parish, drawn to coastal conditions that reminded them of the Adriatic Sea. Developing pioneering equipment and using new harvesting techniques, they were instrumental in establishing Louisiana's oyster industry. Large numbers of Italian immigrants arrived in the state by the turn of the twentieth century, most of them from Sicily. Many settled in New Orleans and its environs, where they would enrich Louisiana's culinary roster further with muffalettos, po'boys (poor boys, po-boys), and St. Joseph's altars— tiered tributes to the Catholic saint arranged with homemade anise and fig cookies, cross-shaped bread, fava beans, and other foods that reminded them of home.

Centuries of cultural fusion have unquestionably shaped Louisiana's food traditions, but another phenomenon has nailed them in place. According to the most recent U.S. Census, there are more native-born residents living in Louisiana than in any other state in the country—around 80 percent. For reasons both economic and emotional, the vast majority of the state's current residents were born here, and that's been true for several generations. Extended families of grandparents, aunts, uncles, and cousins often live in close proximity, meaning a sizable number of young people are privy to the hunting, fishing, and cooking traditions of their forebears. It's easy to learn how to boil crawfish when you're surrounded by adults who perform the rite every spring. Similarly, it's nothing to master your mother's gumbo recipe when she lives down the street. When you're born in a place that has preserved its food traditions so thoroughly and repeats them so seamlessly, everything around you— from legacy restaurants to Cajun *boucheries* to campus tailgate spots—is a vessel for memory, a tether to the past.

Communities around the globe have watched their local food traditions erode, fade, and fight back, but Louisiana's have been surefooted, especially throughout the twentieth century. The king cakes and Mardi Gras parades once limited to French Catholic south Louisiana are now also wildly popular in the historically Protestant parts of the state—central and north Louisiana. The taste for crawfish, formerly confined to the cities and towns around the Atchafalaya Basin, has expanded significantly to include the entire state, as well as pockets of the South. Authentic snoballs, which originated in New Orleans, are now claimed by many other parts of Louisiana. And a fleet of modern food festivals, including the Breaux Bridge Crawfish Festival and the International Rice Festival in Crowley, have enabled dozens of small towns to present a crystal-clear, food-centric identity to the rest of the world.

Climatologists use the term "return frequency" to mark how often documented storms have returned to worldwide locations over time. It helps them understand why a fierce hurricane hurtling toward the coast chooses to land where it lands. But in this storm-prone state, *return frequency* has another meaning—the tug of the culture on anyone who has lived here long enough to feel its effects. I have watched friends come and go over the more than two decades I have lived in Louisiana, and when I ask those who leave what they miss, they reliably point to convivial people and to food traditions not found elsewhere. My friend and fellow freelance journalist Suz Redfearn, who moved to Washington, D.C., in the nineties, once told me, "There's no end to the things I miss about the state, but it's the everyday expectation that food ought to be fun and out of the ordinary that I can't get out of my mind."

Especially during the 1980s and 1990s when Louisiana's economy languished, hordes of young people left the state in search of post-college career opportunities. But as they have grown older and Louisiana has successfully attracted significant new business investment, large numbers of them have returned home. Robbie Trahan, who assisted me with research on the state's rice industry, is one such native. He came back to Louisiana after years of working in Texas to take over operations of his family's Falcon Rice Mill in downtown Crowley. "I knew this way of life didn't exist anywhere else," Trahan said. "And I wanted to raise my kids around it."

He's right. My husband and I have the good fortune of raising our three children in Baton Rouge, and as I watch them shovel in bites of jambalaya and crawfish étouffée around our kitchen table, I try to remind them of their culture's larger significance. *You might live somewhere else one day. But if you do, Louisiana—your home—won't leave your system.* Few places in America feature a culinary identity so well defined and intact.

Louisiana food is vast territory, so it seemed to me that the subject was best channeled through a handful of emblematic ingredients and dishes. The eight chosen in this book highlight diverse aspects of the state's culinary trajectory and how it continues to change. I've started with chapters that explore crawfish and rice—fundamental components of the Louisiana menu whose industries expanded throughout the twentieth century because of the ingenuity of residents. The chapter on Creole cream cheese traces one of the state's legacy dishes, first brought by immigrants adept at making farmhouse cheeses. The beloved breakfast dish experienced a rapid decline in the second half of the twentieth century because of dairy conglomeration and over-regulation, but artisan versions of Creole cream cheese have seen a comeback thanks to the local foods renaissance. Snoballs reveal the manner by which a simple, worldwide confection—sweet syrup over ice—was taken to a high art beginning in the thirties in the city of New Orleans, and how the custom has since seeped into other parts of the state. Filé points to the rich custom of foraging, and to the relationship early immigrants had with the region's first cooks, local Native Americans. The chapter also looks at Louisiana's ritualistic manner of eating. Examining both tamales and jambalaya shows how some Louisiana communities have created identities around dishes that were made by generations of home cooks. A close look at *boudin noir* (Cajun blood sausage) shines a light on a fading aspect of south Louisiana's otherwise robust mom-and-pop country meat markets. Finally, the chapter on oysters celebrates a food that has inspired countless native dishes, and it reveals an industry forced to change in the face of epic coastal erosion. I end each chapter with carefully selected recipes, most of which are mine, developed over many years as a food journalist, active home cook, and Louisiana food champion. They have fed my family and my soul, as I hope they will feed yours.

One could fill volumes with the foods that have been left out, but these provide an entryway into the notable manner by which people in Louisiana have long related to food, the pride with which farmers, fishers, and producers get it to the table, and the way the culinary traditions of this inimitable state continue to evolve.

1

Twist and Separate
Crawfish

The air blowing through the open windows of crawfish farmer Aaron Melancon's pickup truck is cooler than usual for south Louisiana in late March as we pull off onto a dirt road that runs between two of his crawfish ponds. Aaron wants to be sure everything is in order for the upcoming Holy Week—the high point of crawfish season in the state, when people like him work overtime to meet the Easter weekend's soaring demand. He parks near a grove of hardwood trees. As we get out of the truck, one of his workers, a lanky man in chest waders named Juan, approaches from a flat-bottomed boat beached at the edge of one of the ponds. "*Mas pescado?*" Aaron asks him. More fish?

Juan nods. He has spent the morning extracting crawfish from Aaron's neatly arranged pond traps, and he needs to replenish his bait supply. But first, the two men unload several mesh sacks packed with live crawfish from the boat. Standing close to the sacks, I hear the click-clack of tiny claws and feelers through the mesh; their collective noise sounds faintly like trickling water. Aaron and Juan use hand grabbers with smooth metal hooks to grip the thirty-five-pound sacks without tearing them, and they move them to the shade of a large tallow tree. The sacks will remain here briefly until Aaron hauls them to the walk-in cooler at his homestead and workshop a few miles down the road.

Aaron, trim with a tidy goatee, walks to the rear of his pickup. From the bed, he grabs a couple of white plastic drums filled with the frozen parts of two local fish—gizzard shad and Gulf menhaden, or "pogy"—and hands them to Juan. Shad and pogy are the preferred bait among crawfish farmers while the weather is cool; in hotter temperatures, they switch to longer-lasting manmade cylindrical bait pellets. Juan swings the buckets into the boat.

Aaron farms crawfish on 250 disconnected acres of land near the town of Rayne in Louisiana's rice-growing region. The married father of four young children, he is part of a well-established community of farmers who rotate rice and crawfish, two crops that thrive in the same habitat but are harvested in different seasons.

"Crawfish" is, of course, the regional term for crayfish, the ancient fresh-water crustacean found in locations throughout the world and once a significant part of many Old World cuisines. In France, crayfish have been eaten since the Middle Ages. They soared in popularity in the eighteenth century when they were integrated into a wide variety of dishes, including bisque, mousse, and *buisson,* in which whole cooked crayfish were mounted on a tiered dish. They're still eaten in pockets worldwide, but no other state in the nation has embraced them as much as Louisiana.

The United States is home to 338 documented species of crawfish, with the most diversity occurring in the southeast. Thirty–four species have been recorded in the Pelican State, but two dominate the commercial market—the red swamp crawfish, *Procambarus clarkii,* native to the Gulf Coast states, Tennessee, Illinois, and eastern Mexico, and the white river crawfish, *Procambarus zonangulus,* found along the Gulf Coast and up the Mississippi River. Up to 80 percent of the crawfish sold and consumed in Louisiana is *P. clarkii,* a hardy species with more red pigmentation in its shell than *P. zonangulus.* The red swamp crawfish is also known by its rich orange fat, some of which lies tucked inside its carapace, or head. The substance is actually an organ called the *hepatopancreas* that functions like the liver in other animals. Unappealing as it sounds, it doesn't deter serious crawfish fans (me, included) from sucking the head to reach a satisfying blast of fatty, spicy juice. Many go a step further by fishing out the orange substance with the tips or knuckles of their pinkies.

Despite the distribution of crawfish worldwide, the creature has become synonymous with Louisiana thanks to the centuries-old tradition of trapping, selling, and boiling crawfish that was first perfected by the Cajun communities of the Atchafalaya River Basin. The basin is a 140-mile system comprised of bayous, lakes, marshes, and farmland that sprawls from the town of Simmesport, southeast of Alexandria and Marksville, to the Gulf of Mexico. The cradle of Louisiana's Cajun culture, it stretches through fourteen south-central parishes and is the nation's largest river swamp.

The basin provides just the sort of living conditions crawfish love— seasonal flooding and draining, soft mud to burrow in during the sweltering summer, and plenty of natural nooks and crannies on the swamp bottom in which to hide from predators. Crawfish fed generations of indigenous people in Louisiana, and when the Acadians arrived in the mid-eighteenth century after *Le Grand Dérangement*—their deportation from Nova Scotia—they took advantage of the basin's bounty, too.

Crawfish became a reliable springtime food that sustained Cajun families and eventually came to serve as a significant source of income. According to the Louisiana State University Agricultural Center (AgCenter), the nation's first recorded commercial harvest of crawfish, 23,400 pounds caught and sold, came from the Atchafalaya Basin in 1880.

By the 1930s, improved refrigeration and cold storage in the United States helped expand the reach of perishable foods, including crawfish. Consumption of the small crustaceans began to spread from the Atchafalaya basin eastward to Baton Rouge and New Orleans. But the basin wasn't the only place in Louisiana where crawfish were being harvested.

They were plentiful in soggy conditions all over the state, including the growing number of rice fields in the flat Cajun Prairie to the basin's west. Rice farmers who had routinely caught crawfish in their rice fields to boil and eat, learned that if they reflooded the fields after the rice harvest in the fall, they could increase their crawfish population. The flooded fields made for the perfect crawfish winter habitat: the crustaceans feasted on decaying rice plants and small creatures before being harvested in the spring. These weren't commercial operations. Rice farmers simply netted enough to feed their family and friends. Like the Cajun community around the basin, they boiled live crawfish outdoors in washtubs or pots, peeling and eating the tail meat on the spot. Leftover meat was never wasted. It inspired other recipes, namely crawfish étouffée, a straightforward dish combining roux, aromatic vegetables, butter, and crawfish tails, which was served over steamed rice and topped with chopped green onions.

By the first half of the twentieth century, crawfish had become a fixture in songs, paintings, books, and other aspects of art and popular culture in Louisiana, especially around the basin. In 1959, a legislator from Breaux Bridge, east of Lafayette, championed a resolution declaring his town the Crawfish Capital of the World, and a year later the community launched its annual Breaux Bridge Crawfish Festival, which continues today. Another enduring festival began in 1975 when Chalmette, south of New Orleans, created its own Louisiana Crawfish Festival. Both events continue to attract thousands of participants for crawfish-eating contests, crawfish-centric food booths, and live music.

By the middle of the twentieth century, the state's annual crawfish harvest was important enough to politicians, farmers, and agricultural researchers to discuss how to expand it, particularly since the crawfish population ebbed and flowed with the Mississippi River's annual spring floods. In 1950, the Louisiana legislature funded a study to examine the life cycle of crawfish in pond habitats, and by the 1960s, researchers at LSU were applying aquaculture techniques to crawfish, helping Louisiana farmers convert marginal farmland into crawfish ponds. Farmers built levees around their dormant tracts of land, flooded them, and populated the resulting ponds with "brood" or "seed" crawfish. Early harvests didn't yield much, but farmers and researchers eventually learned to improve both water quality and the natural food supply. Before long, intentional crawfish farming was a success. By the mid-1960s, Louisiana farmers had placed about 10,000 acres of farmland in crawfish production, a figure that had risen to more than 180,000 acres by 2014. Louisiana's pond-raised crawfish industry is the largest example of aquaculture in North America in terms of acreage devoted to production.

Pond-raised crawfish proved to be the perfect rotational crop with rice, which was a godsend in Louisiana when rice prices began to drop on the world market in the 1980s. The decline prompted a growing number of rice farmers to permanently integrate crawfish into their operations. It was a natural fit. The infrastructure of ponds, pumps, and canals was already in place for growing rice; farmers needed only to incorporate traps and flat-bottomed crawfish boats. Aaron, who also grows rice and hay, says crawfish farming has been essential for keeping his operations solvent. "I'm not sure what farmers like me would do without crawfish," he says. "Financially, it's a big deal."

⤺

The twentieth century saw a disturbing trend unfolding in the Atchafalaya River Basin. Crawfish production had been slowly declining because of changes in the basin's hydrology brought on by progress and development. In the late 1920s and early 1930s, the U.S. Army Corps of Engineers built flood-control structures that diverted water from the Mississippi River down the Atchafalaya. The diversions were intended to prevent tragedies like the historic flood of the Mississippi in 1927, but redirecting part of the massive river through the basin brought additional sediment, which gradually began to fill in portions of the river swamp. That wasn't all. Pipeline canals, dredged throughout the basin by oil and gas and timber companies for exploration and transport, also upset the basin's natural flow. Over the last several decades, one of the Atchafalaya's great struggles has been the loss of swampland where crawfish have traditionally thrived. Water levels in many places are now too low for crawfishermen to access with boats. The Army Corps of Engineers continues to manage intricate flood control, navigation, and fresh-water distribution systems in the basin, some of which present ongoing challenges to the crawfish industry. Moreover, many young people whose parents and grandparents crawfished in this majestic corner of Louisiana are discontinuing the family tradition because of its high cost, variable conditions, and intense labor.

"The oil companies' and Corps of Engineers' canals and drainage projects have dried up three-quarters of the original swamp and we're losing ground fast," says Dean Wilson, executive director of the non-profit Atchafalaya Basinkeeper. "Crawfishermen are frustrated. It used to be the way they would make a lot of their money in the spring to pay bills, repair boats, and get ready for other fishing seasons, and it's just not that way anymore."

Jody Meche has crawfished in the basin all his life. His father, who also crawfished, grew up on a houseboat in the swamp and didn't move to the nearby town of Henderson until he was a young adult. Jody is a self-described jack-of-all-trades who supplements his springtime crawfish income by shrimping, skinning alligators, and sometimes working as a journeyman in the oil and gas industry (he points out the irony). Jody tells me that basin crawfishermen have a completely different experience than crawfish farmers. They have to understand conditions in the wild enough to know where to drop their lines and place their cylindrical mesh traps.

In the spring, Jody gets in his boat and crawfishes all over the basin, testing sections for activity in the open water or in coves under moss-draped trees by setting a few traps. Basin crawfish traps are long and barrel-shaped so they can reach into deeper water. If the yield looks promising in a given spot, Jody sets more traps and comes back a day or two later to empty them, loading the crawfish into sacks on his boat. He brings the catch to a middleman. The challenges with basin crawfishing don't stop with the loss of habitat, says Jody: the price per pound earned by crawfishermen often can't keep up with the cost of doing business. "Here in the basin, it's a beautiful way of life. I love to fish and it's in my roots," he says. "But between bait and gas, a man can hardly make a living."

❦

Today, the state's $150 million crawfish industry produces an average of 80 million pounds of crawfish every year, the vast majority of it from ponds. The growth of the pond industry has allowed producers to keep up with demand for crawfish, which has grown substantially both within and outside of Louisiana. Farming has also expanded the crawfish season. Wild crawfish from the basin hit in large numbers between April and June, but pond-raised crawfish are harvested in earnest between February and June, and sometimes as early as December. The longer season has introduced an expectation, especially in heavily Catholic south Louisiana, that crawfish will be plentiful during Lent, and especially over Easter weekend, no matter when the holiday happens to fall. Aaron and other statewide producers will put in their longest hours of the year during Holy Week, returning to ponds that they ordinarily fish every other day as much as twice a day. Their efforts are worth it. The price per pound for crawfish is at its highest then; after Easter it begins to drop.

It's easy to spot crawfish ponds along Louisiana's network of interstates, highways, and rural back roads. A crawfish pond has no standard size, but most are rectangular and between ten and forty acres each. They're only about eighteen inches deep, so the aluminum boats that farmers use to reach their traps actually push their way through the water with the help of rear-mounted hydraulic wheels or raised outboard motors that have been adapted to shallow water. Beginning in the winter, you start to see the red, orange, and white plastic necks of crawfish traps protruding from the glassy surface. Underneath, these triangular cages are fixed to the muddy pond bottom with small spikes. Crawfish crawl in through an entrance funnel in the mesh to dine on the bait inside, and a day or two later, the farmer hauls up traps one by one and dumps the catch onto a sacking table in the boat.

Aaron and I join Juan as he backs the boat into the awaiting pond and motors to the first trap on the closest row. While steering with his left hand, he baits an empty trap with his right. When the boat reaches the submerged trap, he switches the two traps, placing the baited one in the water and dumping the contents of the other onto the sacking table. A pound of so of crawfish skitter on the surface in front of him, their claws and feelers scratching audibly as they find their bearings. Some still cling to a pogy carcass, its bones nearly picked clean. Juan baits the now-empty cage with a fish head just as the boat reaches the next trap on the row. He plunges it into the water, lifting and dumping the submerged trap in quick succession. The process continues until every trap on the pond has been emptied, baited, and replaced. The boat never stops moving, and I am mesmerized by Juan's steady pace.

Backyard crawfish boils and their endless piles of scarlet crustaceans are the epitome of plenty in Louisiana, but that image doesn't square with the scant amount of crawfish typically gathered from each trap. Farmers can count on only about a pound at a time, so they have to work fast to meet the season's relentless demand. Juan's arms move steadily, and it doesn't take long before the sacking table in front of him is full of ruddy crawfish rearing their pinchers and crawling backward across the slick surface. The colloquialism "to crawfish" means to welsh or back out, and it makes sense when you look at the animal's characteristic tail-first strategy, its eyes peering upward suspiciously as it moves in reverse. The sacking table has four chutes onto which purple or green mesh sacks are attached, and as the pile of crawfish grows, the creatures are forced to tumble down the chutes into the sacks below.

Aaron's traps are set thirty-six feet apart in the water, tighter than the average forty- to sixty-foot intervals used by most producers. He arranges them in an alternating red and orange color pattern, which helps his workers recognize when a trap is missing. Sometimes they're toppled by herons or egrets, and occasionally they are stolen by locals. The color coding is an extra step, but one that helps cut down on replacement costs.

While referred to as aquaculture, the way crawfish are raised on ponds in Louisiana is more about encouraging a creature to thrive in an existing habitat that it already likes—the rice farm. Traditionally, rice farmers in Louisiana would drain their fields and the crawfish would just be there, says Aaron, who grew up in Roberts Cove, a rice-growing community near Rayne established in the late nineteenth century by German immigrants.

This two-crop pond system begins when farmers plant rice seeds in the spring, usually between March and April. When the rice plants sprout and are firmly set a few weeks later, farmers flood the fields using electric- or diesel-powered pumps and a system of underground pipes. This is known as the "permanent flood" since the water level will remain steady until just before the rice is harvested in August or September. A few weeks after the permanent flood, the farmer stocks the pond with adult brood crawfish, about forty to fifty pounds per acre. There are no hatcheries in crawfish farming. A producer simply gathers crawfish from one of his other ponds or another farmer, or he nets them from the basin.

The brood crawfish mate in open water. When the farmer drains the fields to prepare for the rice harvest, the crawfish move to the pond's surrounding levees to burrow in the mud, where females lay their eggs and cap off the burrows with mud plugs that they can't remove themselves without the help of a hard rain. While underground, females lay about two to six hundred eggs each. The birthrate is lower than that of either shrimp or oysters, but the survival rate for baby crawfish is high.

While the crawfish are tucked in their burrows, the farmer refloods the pond around early October to encourage stubble from harvested rice to grow. This reflooding, combined with a good hard autumn rain, softens the mud plugs and allows the crawfish to push their way out of the burrow. Young crawfish are attached to the swimmerets beneath their mother's abdomen; after a brief period of molting and getting used to life in the open water, they scoot away from their mother and begin to live on their own. There is plenty of food, even though crawfish ponds are never sprinkled with feed. Instead, farmers create a nutrient-rich food web whose base is decaying rice plants. The detritus from the plants attracts microorganisms that in turn attract larger creatures. The crawfish feast on a natural buffet that includes plant and insect matter, worms, larvae, micro-crustaceans, and occasionally small vertebrae like minnows and tadpoles. Juvenile crawfish reach harvest size in about five months, usually around February. But these aren't the first crawfish to emerge in the Louisiana crawfish season. Mono-cropping operations, where only crawfish are raised, can send crawfish to market as early as December or January. By June, the temperatures have warmed up enough to force the crawfish on farms and in the basin to begin burrowing out of sight into the cool, soft mud.

Farming has created predictable conditions that have helped expand the supply of crawfish, but pond productivity is still dramatically affected by Mother Nature. When crawfish season rolls around, the conversation among crawfish producers, chefs, merchants, home cooks, and crawfish fans concerns the season's expected quality and quantity. The weather, they all know, plays a big role. A dry summer one year will indeed lower the birthrate in the following spring because it impedes the ability of the crawfish to dig deep and bear their young in the mud. And a well-timed rainfall in the fall is essential for softening the mud plugs that allow crawfish families to ease out and find food. Without rain, they lay trapped below where there is little to eat, increasing the mortality of the hatchlings inside the burrow.

Back on Aaron's boat, Juan pilots down the last lane and empties and rebaits the final trap. He beaches the boat on the levee and loads the sacks of crawfish onto the bed of the pickup. Aaron and I jump in the truck's cab and head for his workshop.

The manager of a Chinese restaurant in a nearby town is waiting for Aaron in the driveway. In the spring, it's not unusual for a tray of boiled crawfish to sit beside sesame chicken and broccoli beef at an Asian buffet in Cajun Country and throughout parts of Louisiana. And even if they don't serve boiled crawfish, Chinese restaurants throughout the state often use crawfish in some dishes that call for chicken or shrimp. Aaron hands over a couple of sacks in exchange for a check, and the restaurant manager drives off.

Live crawfish make up most of the sales of Louisiana crawfish, but about 10 percent of the annual crop—usually comprised of smaller crawfish—are sold as peeled, deveined, parboiled packaged tail meat. A handful of processing plants in the state perform this function, which, remarkably, still takes place by hand. A few prototype peeling machines have been introduced over the years, but various glitches have kept them from being commercialized. Instead, workers gather round tables in a processing plant—not unlike guests at a crawfish boil—delicately extracting the tail meat from the shell and tossing the morsels into large aluminum bowls.

In the 1990s, the Louisiana crawfish industry faced a slowdown in consumer sales due to imported crawfish tails. Packages of processed tail meat from China and Spain were entering the Louisiana market at significantly cheaper prices per pound than local tail meat. Eager to save a buck in a period that predated the local foods movement, Louisiana consumers and restaurant chefs alike scooped up the less expensive product, and regional producers watched their sales plummet. The imported tails particularly affected the state's crawfish-peeling industry, which lodged a formal complaint with the federal government. In March 1997, the U.S. Commerce Department ruled that Chinese crawfish tails had indeed been illegally dumped onto the U.S. market for less than fair-market value. The government instituted a tariff on the Chinese product, bringing the cost closer in line with Louisiana crawfish tails and helping to resuscitate the state's crawfish processors, which had been on the brink of collapse.

Ironically, the Chinese crawfish that wreaked havoc on the Louisiana industry in the nineties is the same species extolled in the state,

P. clarkii, the celebrated red swamp crawfish. Introduced in Europe, Asia, Africa, and parts of the United States other than Louisiana, the red swamp crawfish is considered by most to be an invasive, destructive nuisance whose disease resistance and ability to adapt has helped it choke out other species, including native species of crawfish, in other parts of the world. Louisianans understand destructive invaders: nutria, water hyacinth, and Asian carp—all introduced in the state—have toyed with the ecology of the Louisiana's fragile swamps and waterways for decades. But it's not widely known by crawfish aficionados here that their signature crustacean is regarded by much of the rest of the world as an intractable pest.

Aaron tries to sell directly to consumers as often as possible—profits are better—but a good portion of his harvest goes to distributors and on to seafood markets in Louisiana, Texas, and Arkansas. During the season, many of these markets sell thousands of pounds of boiled and live crawfish a week to eager consumers. Tony's Seafood in Baton Rouge is one of the largest such markets. Founded in 1959, this iconic retailer has operated from north Baton Rouge for most of its existence. The neighborhood surrounding Tony's was once dominated by middle-class plant workers employed at local refineries and chemical companies, but as they flocked to new suburbs in the 1960s and 1970s, the area saw investment stagnate and experienced a continual increase in poverty and crime. Still, Tony's remains a huge draw for patrons throughout greater Baton Rouge. Outside, the parking lot gets so busy that Tony's owners pay an off-duty officer to direct cars; inside, Tony's employees are trained to organize lines of patrons with Disney World–like efficiency. They hurriedly fill orders of crawfish to keep the line moving, scooping steaming, boiled crawfish into large plastic sacks, plopping them onto scales, and handing them over. Customers grab packages of boiled corn and new potatoes from an aluminum kiosk on their way to the checkout lines, often leaving with enough food to feed dozens of friends and family. During Easter weekend, the store will sell about 100,000 pounds of live and boiled crawfish over a two-day period.

Markets like Tony's and grocery stores throughout the state also sell packages of tail meat, which rose in popularity after the peeling industry took root in the 1960s. With packaged tail meat more available, Louisianans expanded the way they cooked and consumed crawfish. The best-known and most widely prepared recipe using tail meat is crawfish étouffée, but that's just the tip of the iceberg. Tails are deep-fried and tossed with honey mustard dressing on spinach salad, turned into party dips, baked in cornbread, incorporated in boudin, and stuffed in mushrooms or enchiladas. We form them into pan-fried cakes, bake them in savory pies, combine them with cream sauce and ladle them over pasta or fresh fish, and toss them in gumbos, chowders, bisques, soups, and stews.

The springtime New Orleans Jazz and Heritage Festival is considered a mecca of Cajun and Creole food, and crawfish is the central ingredient of some of the fest's most popular dishes. Long lines snake from the booth where Marksville-based Panorama Foods sells crawfish bread, a wedge of dough stuffed with gooey cheddar and mozzarella cheeses, crawfish tails, and spices and baked until firm and brown. It's my personal favorite. A few booths down, the veteran Chalmette caterer Patton's serves crawfish beignets, puffs of crawfish tail meat and breading that are deep fried and topped with white remoulade sauce. Patton's also sells crawfish sacks, a moist mix of crawfish tails, breading, and spices, twisted in a pastry sheet, tied off with a green onion sliver, and fried until crisp. Patton's famed three-item combo plate has been served since the company began participating in Jazz Fest in 1989 and includes these two items along with the oyster patty, a flaky pastry cup soused in a gravy-like oyster reduction.

The best-known crawfish dish at Jazz Fest is Crawfish Monica, crawfish tails in a spicy cream and wine sauce served over rotini pasta, the creation of Kajun Kettle Foods president and chef Pierre Hilzim, who named it for his wife and business partner, Monica Davidson. The company estimates that between 1983 (when the booth opened) and 2013 it served about one million bowls of Crawfish Monica.

Louisiana's broad range of crawfish dishes also includes the cozy, handheld crawfish pie, and on my drive back to Baton Rouge from Rayne after visiting Aaron, I seek one out. I stop at Billy's, one of several Cajun meat markets in the town of Scott near Lafayette. Billy's is best known for its hulking boudin balls, but it also sells a mean single-serving crawfish pie. Gripping it in a grease-stained miniature brown paper bag, I bite into the sturdy, crescent-shaped crust. A puff of steam escapes. The pastry holds a juicy mixture of sautéed crawfish tails, red and green pepper, onions, and garlic; with each bite, the bounty threatens to escape. It demands quick eating, like a melting ice cream cone in the heat. I'm happy to oblige.

⤳

A few days later, on Good Friday, my husband John, our three children, and I drive to Alexandria, Louisiana, where John's mother and extended family live. His kinfolk are part of a larger community of Belgian immigrants who made their way from Flanders to central Louisiana to farm in the late nineteenth century. Driving north on I-49 near the town of Lecompte, we look out onto an expanse of crawfish ponds. Egrets on stilt-like legs meander through the water, taking advantage of a free meal. The steady growth of the crawfish industry over the last fifty years has helped the culture spread further into central and north Louisiana and, to a smaller extent, to other Gulf Coast states.

John's family has bought four sacks of live crawfish—about 120 pounds—from a local market. The serving size per person for boiled crawfish is four to five pounds, so we have enough to feed the adults and children expected. One corner of my mother-in-law's woodsy backyard has been designated as the boiling area. Our kids, Marien, Christopher, and Mercer, and their cousins are warned to steer clear of the two gas-powered burners that will soon bring large pots of water to a rolling boil.

Like much of outdoor cooking in Louisiana, boiling crawfish is a responsibility that remains in the grip of the patriarchy. John's uncle

Louis "Cooter" Marien and family friends Hal Bailey and Carl "Rolie" Verzwyvelt are organizing the process. On a rickety card table, they have arranged onions, lemons, garlic heads, cartons of salt, and one-pound sacks of dry crawfish boil, a spice mixture that includes cayenne pepper, salt, garlic powder, onion powder, and other spices. After the water is seasoned with these ingredients and comes to a boil, the men will lower baskets filled with live crawfish into it. At different points, they'll also toss in new potatoes and mini-ears of corn on the cob, white button mushrooms, and smoked pork sausage. Corn and potatoes are requisite accompaniments at any backyard boil, but statewide crawfish boilers these days also incorporate artichokes, cauliflower, edamame, and other personal flourishes.

Before the cooking begins in earnest, the children reach into a large washtub that holds the live crawfish, freed from their sacks and sprayed with water to wash off any remaining mud. I watch them grab the creatures gingerly from behind, avoiding contact with searching pinchers. They place them in the grass to watch them race, a long-standing family tradition.

Anyone who boils crawfish in Louisiana claims a signature preparation technique, and part of the boiling ritual is both discussing and defending it. Rolie, Cooter, and Hal share the belief that crawfish should be "purged" in salt for extra cleaning before they're boiled, and they like to use dry seasonings and salt rather than liquid crawfish boil. But they don't always agree on the order or amount of the seasonings, and occasionally, I overhear annoyed tones and the push and pull of competing philosophies.

When the water is at a rolling boil, they lower the baskets of live crawfish into the pots. After the water returns to a boil, they extinguish the flames on the burners and let the crawfish cook and soak up the flavor for about twenty minutes. Then they slowly, carefully raise the baskets, dump the boiled crawfish into clean ice chests, and allow them to cool for a few minutes (this is when some boilers, including producer Aaron Melancon, shake sacks of fiery dry seasoning onto the cooked creatures).

We move like locusts to the ice chests, using a red Solo cup to scoop the crawfish onto round plastic lap trays adorned with pictures of happy crawfish. Everyone takes a seat, and we hover over our piles for a moment, plotting which mudbug to pick up first. Then we twist the joint between the head and tail, neatly separating the two. Some of us suck the juices from the head before tossing it onto the discard pile. To reach the tail meat, I wind away the first coil of the shell, making it easier to pop the meat free as I push it up from the tail's base. We parents peel tails for our children, who are still mastering their speed and efficiency. The piles of expended heads and shells grow. Between savoring the tail meat, we bite into mini ears of corn and whole new potatoes. There is no need for utensils. Rolls of paper towels sit in the center of each table, and when we try to grab a sheet neatly, we leave behind trails of orange fingerprints. The crawfish fat and the cooking liquid have coated our fingers with residue. We warn the children not to touch anything, especially their eyes, until they wash their hands.

Blessedly, it will be awhile before we're sated. So without guilt, we go back for more.

Crawfish Étouffée

Crawfish étouffée, or "smothered" crawfish, is the quintessential crawfish dish. This stew-like fare became popular in Louisiana in the mid-twentieth century, when crawfish—and crawfish tails—were more widely available in the state. Like gumbo and red beans and rice, crawfish étouffée has been made by generations of home cooks without regard to rigid rules. Recipes have appeared in countless Louisiana community cookbooks, where the general formula combines butter or another fat, aromatic vegetables, crawfish tails, liquid, and dry seasonings to create a "stew" served over rice. From there, the recipes branch off in different directions to include a range of ingredients that thicken the mixture and add flavor. The family recipe of food writer and St. Martin Parish native Marcelle Bienvenu uses cornstarch and water to create a slurry; other cooks add a few tablespoons of light roux. Tomato sauce, Rotel tomatoes, beer, wine, or mushrooms are also fairly common enhancers. In his *New Yorker* essay "Missing Links"—one of several dispatches that document the writer's enthusiasm for Louisiana food—Calvin Trillin mentions the secret, anti-gourmet ingredient in the crawfish étouffée recipe of his New Iberia friend James Edmunds: a can of cream of mushroom soup.

I like a simple, unfussy étouffée with minimal ingredients and lots of crawfish tails. I make this recipe throughout the spring, but I especially like to make it in June, when the price of crawfish tails has fallen considerably and when the bright green bell peppers in my kitchen garden are ready for harvest.

Serves 8.

4 tablespoons (half a stick) butter
1 large green bell pepper, diced
1 celery stalk, diced
1 large yellow onion, diced

2 tablespoons roux (see below)
1 cup water or chicken or shellfish stock, divided
2 one-pound packages peeled Louisiana crawfish tails
⅛ teaspoon cayenne pepper
Salt and ground black pepper
Hot, cooked white rice for serving
¼ cup chopped green onions (green parts only) for garnish
¼ cup chopped fresh parsley for garnish

Melt butter in a large skillet over medium heat. Add bell pepper, celery, and yellow onion, and sauté until soft. Add roux and half of water and whisk until thoroughly incorporated. Add crawfish tails and cook until tails curl, about 5 minutes. Add cayenne pepper, salt, and black pepper to taste. Add remaining ½ cup water and simmer 15–20 minutes. Add more liquid if necessary to reach a stew-like consistency. Serve over rice and top with green onions and parsley.

Roux

Roux springs from French cuisine and is the combination of flour and fat, browned to different degrees and used to thicken dishes. In Cajun and Creole cuisine, roux is generally taken to a medium to dark brown hue, depending on the dish you're concocting. There's an art to reaching a darker shade without burning it. Roux is highly personal—there are as many opinions on its correct assembly as there are cooks who prepare it. Here's my tried and true method.

½ cup vegetable oil
½ cup all-purpose flour

In a heavy-bottomed saucepan or skillet, heat vegetable oil to medium high. Sprinkle flour in oil and whisk to combine. Whisk or stir with a flat-edged wooden spoon constantly so that mixture does not burn.

Roux should be light brown, or the color of peanut butter, in about 10 minutes. For a dark brown roux, cook 5 more minutes. If roux browns too quickly, remove from heat for a minute or two. When it reaches desired color, remove from heat entirely and set aside, or continue with recipe. Refrigerate for one week or freeze for three months.

Crawfish Cornbread

While crawfish étouffée highlights two local ingredients, crawfish and rice, crawfish cornbread gives the crustacean a chance to pair with the state's only true indigenous grain, corn. Corn and cornmeal were instrumental in filling the bellies of native people, colonists, and residents in general over the course of the state's history. Here, yellow cornmeal hosts sumptuous crawfish tails, fresh corn, onions and peppers, spices, and gooey cheese. This flavor-packed bread makes a rich accompaniment to a steaming bowl of gumbo, but it is also delicious on its own or served with a simple salad. In Louisiana, "crawfish cornbread" can also sometimes mean soft cornbread dressing studded with crawfish tails.

Serves 6.

 1 ½ cups yellow cornmeal
 1 cup all-purpose flour
 ¼ cup sugar (optional)
 2 ¼ teaspoons baking powder
 1 ½ teaspoons salt
 ½ teaspoon garlic powder
 ¼ teaspoon cayenne pepper
 2 eggs
 1 cup milk
 ¼ cup sour cream
 ¼ cup vegetable oil
 2 pounds Louisiana crawfish tail meat (1 pound works, too, but
    2 tastes better)
 1 cup fresh corn kernels, scraped from the cob (about 3 ears), or
    frozen corn kernels, thawed
 1 ½ cups grated pepper Jack cheese
 ½ cup chopped yellow onion
 ½ cup chopped red bell pepper

Preheat oven to 350 degrees F and grease or spray a 9x13-inch baking dish. In a large bowl, combine cornmeal, flour, sugar, baking powder, salt, garlic powder, and cayenne pepper. In a separate medium-sized bowl, combine eggs, milk, sour cream, and oil. Pour wet ingredients into dry ingredients and gently combine. Add crawfish tails, corn, cheese, onion, and bell pepper. Combine well, but do not overmix.

Pour batter into prepared pan and bake for 45 minutes. Let rest 10 minutes and cut into squares.

Crawfish Fennel Salad with Tangy Vinaigrette

Crawfish tails are most associated with assertive, belly-warming dishes, but they are also perfect for light, summer seafood salads. This recipe pairs the naturally sweet flavor of crawfish tails with the anise notes of fennel and the fresh crunch of celery and red and yellow bell peppers.

Serves 4–6.

2 tablespoons olive oil
½ cup finely diced yellow onion
1 pound Louisiana crawfish tails
Salt and ground black pepper
1 cup chopped yellow pepper
1 cup chopped red pepper
½ cup chopped celery
½ cup thinly sliced fennel bulb
½ cup canned hearts of palm slices

Dressing:

¼ cup red wine vinegar
3 tablespoons Dijon mustard
3 tablespoons lemon juice
4 tablespoons honey
1 teaspoon celery seed
½ cup olive oil
Salt and ground pepper

For serving:

4 cups chopped lettuce
2 ripe tomatoes, sliced

12 basil leaves, rolled and cut into ribbons (chiffonade)
4–6 lemon wedges

Heat olive oil in a skillet over medium heat, and sauté onion until translucent. Add crawfish tails, with fat, and sauté for about 5 minutes, or until the meat is thoroughly cooked and tails curl. Remove from heat immediately and season with salt and ground pepper to taste. Set aside.

In a large bowl, combine yellow and red bell peppers, celery, fennel, and hearts of palm. Set aside.

Prepare dressing by adding vinegar, mustard, lemon juice, honey, and celery seed to a food processor. Combine, and while blade is turning, slowly add oil. Season to taste with salt and ground pepper.

Add crawfish tails to the bowl with the raw, chopped veggies. Pour ½ cup of the dressing into the bowl and toss well to combine. Reserve remainder of dressing for another use. Let the salad marinate in the refrigerator for a few hours or overnight. Serve over cold lettuce and garnish with sliced tomatoes, basil ribbons, and lemon wedges.

2

The Rice Has to Pop
Jambalaya

Every year on Memorial Day weekend, the city of Gonzales hosts a four-day festival devoted to the one-pot rice dish people here in Ascension Parish have been preparing for generations: jambalaya. Thousands gather for carnival rides, live music, and for a grueling outdoor cooking contest unabashedly named the World Jambalaya Cook-Off. In the late May south Louisiana heat, mostly male teams of two prepare their best chicken jambalaya in regulation cast-iron pots over open hardwood fires (gas burners aren't allowed). Almost all contestants come from families with deep roots in the community, and many are the sons, nephews, and cousins of past winners. Hopefuls begin preparing for the cook-off months before, fine-tuning equipment, reviewing their order of assembly, and mastering exactly how much fire is required to cook a large amount of rice without burning it.

A few weeks before the cook-off, I called Jody Elisar, a former champion and current judge, and asked if we could meet. I wanted to pick his brain about why jambalaya is so important to the people of Gonzales, and what it takes to prepare a version that would pass muster here. At first blush, jambalaya seems simple and straightforward. Its short ingredient list has made it Louisiana's most ubiquitous large-group dish, cheaper than crawfish étouffée and easier to serve than gumbo. It's a fixture at football tailgate parties, family gatherings, school functions, state fairs and festivals, cafeteria lunches, rural wedding receptions, church dinners, and on-the-spot fundraisers for sports teams and youth groups. All it takes to prepare the Cajun version—the kind made in Gonzales— is a pot and three main ingredients: rice, water, and a protein or two of choice.

But to the people of Ascension Parish, there is a right way to cook Cajun jambalaya—and plenty of wrong ways. Mastering the dish takes years of practice, the right equipment, and a keen sense of fire management.

Jody took a break from his day as an industrial equipment salesman and met me for lunch at a rural restaurant about twenty miles southeast of Baton Rouge in the town of Burnside. He learned to cook jambalaya as a kid, at his uncle's knee, and first entered the cook-off as a teenager. After eighteen tries, he finally won in 2008. The field of contestants, he says, is stacked with experienced outdoor jambalaya cooks, and everyone cooks at the top of their game. The judges, therefore, are exceptionally critical. As they sample forkfuls of the sturdy rice dish from numbered Styrofoam boxes, they look for the slightest imperfections. The stakes are high; Jody's championship stature helped him start a sideline career as a large-scale caterer that includes preparing jambalaya for events associated with the LSU football team. He also launched his own line of instant jambalaya mix.

Jambalaya is on the menu of the restaurant we've chosen, but Jody has no plans to order it. Many restaurants use parboiled rice in their jambalaya—rice that has been steamed and dried during the milling process, helping it cook uniformly and separately. Busy casual restaurants love parboiled rice, but Jody considers it too dummy-proofed to be interesting. I order the dish anyway because I want him to analyze it.

A lean man with a quick smile, Jody brims with enthusiasm as we begin to talk about jambalaya. The dish is claimed by the entire state, but it is especially revered around Gonzales. It's not because rice tra-ditionally was grown here—on the contrary, this is historic sugarcane country—but rather because of the frequency with which it was made in local kitchens throughout the twentieth century. Rice was an affordable staple in this largely rural area, and since many people kept livestock and hunted, they always had some sort of meat on hand.

The origins of jambalaya are most likely in New Orleans. Between 1763 and 1800, Spain held most of the Louisiana colony, and Spanish immigrants poured into New Orleans, then the Louisiana capital, where their food traditions fused with those of the French, African slaves, and Native Americans. Paella—the common one-pot rice dish from Valencia made with shellfish, sausage, and saffron—would have been replicable in Louisiana since rice had become a common staple. (Decades earlier, colonists and slaves had begun growing so-called "providence" rice by scattering seeds along riverbanks and bayous and harvesting what grew.) Since saffron wasn't available in Louisiana, the flavor of this modified paella was enhanced by salt, black and red pepper, and chicken and pork fat. The name "jambalaya" stems from the French word for ham, *jambon,* one of the meats originally used to give the new dish flavor and heft.

Two of Louisiana's oldest documented cookbooks feature recipes for jambalaya. The Christian Woman's Exchange's *Creole Cookery,* published in New Orleans in 1885, includes "jumballaya, a Spanish Creole dish," in its section on vegetables. The recipe advises soaking a pound of rice for an hour and then combining the rice in a pot with hot water and cold roast chicken, or slices of turkey and ham that have been fried in lard. Highlighting the dish's adaptability, the cookbook also states that oysters and shrimp can be substituted for the pork and poultry.

Lafcadio Hearn's *La Cuisine Creole,* a compilation of popular recipes from New Orleans chefs and home cooks (also published in 1885 in the Crescent City), features another version. Hearn suggests combining "a stewed fowl, raw rice, a slice of ham minced, and pepper and salt." He credits local Indians for its origins, remarks that southern children are fond of it, and says it can be made of many things. But what stands out most about Hearn's instructions is this cautionary note: "Let all cook together until the rice swells and absorbs all the gravy of the stewed chicken, but it must not be allowed to get hard or dry."

One hundred and forty years later, many jambalaya enthusiasts—especially those from Gonzales—would agree that the dish succeeds or fails by the texture of its rice. This is exactly the sort of thing I want to talk to Jody about.

Jambalaya migrated fifty miles up the Mississippi River from New Orleans to Ascension Parish, where generations of mothers and grandmothers made it over stoves in home kitchens. More often, though, men in the area prepared it in cast-iron pots outdoors over open fires. Jambalaya has been such a part of the local culture of this area that in 1967, community leaders convinced then–Louisiana governor John J. McKeithen to pass a resolution declaring Gonzales the "Jambalaya Capital of the World." Local organizers planned an annual festival for the following year to further substantiate their claim.

From the first, organizers included a cook-off on the festival agenda, and the event quickly became the gathering place for celebrating the tradition publicly. Certain families in town became known for their jambalaya cooking skills, and year after year, these families would field contestants, as the townspeople gathered to watch. Recently, the cook-off has also become serious business. The champion earns a cash prize and, like Miss America and her post-pageant road tour, he (or she) represents the Jambalaya Festival Association throughout the ensuing year. The winner cooks for two public events and usually parlays the exposure into professional catering gigs.

Jambalaya, like vegetable soup, chili, or gumbo, is one of those dishes often assembled by gut; it's a template for creativity. Home cooks prepare jambalaya with a variety of meats and seafood, although chicken and pork are the most common ingredients because of their natural fat content and because their browning ability contributes to jambalaya's signature caramel color. Sometimes crawfish jambalaya appears during crawfish season. And around New Orleans, red or Creole jambalaya, made with tomato paste, tomato sauce or fresh tomatoes, and shrimp or oysters, is also popular. But at the Gonzales cook-off, contestants are confined to specific ingredients: chicken, long-grain rice, cooking oil, and their choice of yellow onions, green onions, fresh or granulated garlic, bell peppers, celery, cayenne pepper, black pepper, salt, and hot sauce. (The rules specify "red" hot sauce only.) To make sure no one adds bootlegged ingredients, organizers deliver a package of approved groceries to each contestant at his or her cooking station thirty minutes before the heats begin. This standardization creates relative consistency among the completed dishes, allowing the judges to focus more on technique than creativity.

Each contestant has his own method of cooking outdoor jambalaya, but generally the process unfolds similarly at each station. The teams begin by building a fire, using freshly cut firewood from the piles that organizers have arranged. Once a fire has burned down to a level the cook likes, he arranges his trusty, seasoned black iron pot over the flames and coals, and then he adds cooking oil. When the oil is hot enough, in goes bone-in, skin-on chicken pieces and aromatic vegetables, which the contestants have been busy chopping. The order of ingredients varies from team to team, but once the vegetables and meat have browned and some of the oil removed, the cooks add long-grain white rice, water, and dry seasonings. They stir their cauldrons with long paddles and then cover them with large aluminum lids. Occasionally, they take the lids off and stir the rice quickly to ensure each grain cooks evenly and is coated with flavor. The finished product is a loose, but slightly sticky amalgam of tender, seasoned rice, braised chicken fallen off the bone, flecks of spices, and bits of aromatic vegetables that have melted into everything else.

Over the last several decades, the cook-off has drawn more contestants and become more regimented. Teams can't confer with anyone while they're cooking, nor can the crowd approach them. Police barricades border the area where spectators stand, and a twenty-foot no-man's-land of grass comes between the spectators and the cooking stations. Jody, gobbling up bites of cold shrimp and iceberg lettuce salad, tells me that entries are judged blind on appearance, taste, and texture. Numerical scores are tabulated in a computer program developed specifically for the cook-off by a local technology firm.

Over the years, Gonzales has created its own language and measuring stick for describing what a good batch of Cajun jambalaya should look and taste like. Jody tells me the overall color should resemble a brown paper bag. And when presented to the judges, the dish should be free of what he calls "floating trash," that is, overcooked bits of chicken, rice, or vegetables. The flavor of a successful jambalaya is balanced—if it's too salty or spicy it will lose points immediately. Authentic jambalaya is intended to be more nuanced. The rice should have absorbed plenty of natural flavor from the chicken and from the aromatic vegetables and dry spices, and the chicken itself should be browned and tender.

"But what's really important," says Jody seriously, "is that the rice has to pop."

In all my years of covering food in Louisiana, I've only heard this description of finished rice once before. I ask him to explain it further, and he pauses. He reaches for the blue pen I'm using to scribble notes and finds a white paper napkin ring unfurled near his plate. He flattens the paper and with head bent low begins to sketch a small picture. When he's done, he slides it across the table toward me. I'm looking at a cartoonish image of a grain of rice whose top and bottom are split into V-shapes. Down the body of the grain is a line that looks like a thin zipper. The picture resembles a headless creature with arms and legs outstretched jubilantly.

I peer at Jody, and he nods. "It has to absorb enough water and heat to expand and pop on the ends and get a seam down the middle," he says. "If it looks like this, you got it right."

Popped rice, according to jambalaya experts in Gonzales, is the insider symbol that your rice has cooked the right amount; it's not under- or overdone. If the grain cooks too fast over heat that's too high, it becomes dry and brittle, as Hearn warned. If it's cooked too long or is stirred too much, the grains end up splitting down the middle entirely.

Jody draws an example of two separate, slightly bowed half-grains whose texture will lack the heft of a full grain. Splitting happens when a cook stirs the pot too much. "You *cannot* overwork the rice," Jody says. "I tell people you have to think of the grains like kids at a spend-the-night party. Check on them carefully. Don't get them too riled up."

⤳

If the treatment of rice was the inflexible secret to cooking jambalaya, I wanted to understand more about rice itself. Rice is, of course, the backbone of both Creole and Cajun cuisines and a critical component of Louisiana's hallmark dishes. Gumbo is not gumbo without rice. Neither is crawfish étouffée, turtle sauce piquant, shrimp Creole, redfish court-bouillon, boudin, red beans and rice, dirty rice, or the rice dressing that sits on so many holiday tables next to its cornbread counterpart. The ultimate meal stretcher, rice has helped generations of Louisianans provide for their own families and welcome extra guests to the table. It is the connective tissue running through the state's native dishes.

Indigenous to Asia and consumed by humans as far back as 5,000 B.C., rice reportedly made its way to the American colonies in 1685. Its first stop was South Carolina. According to that state's Department of Agriculture, a boat captain named John Thurber arrived in Charleston on a vessel from Madagascar and gave the rice seeds he had collected there to a man named Henry Woodward, the first English settler in the South Carolina colony. Woodward planted some of the seeds and gave the rest to friends who did the same. Known as Carolina Gold, the variety grew successfully and helped the state kick off its rice industry. By 1696, South Carolina's commercial harvest was underway. Rice would soon spread to other parts of the colonies, including Louisiana, and probably also trickled in from slave ships after they began arriving in earnest in 1716.

Rice was grown informally in Louisiana until the late nineteenth century, when German immigrants in Acadia Parish began to cultivate it. They had moved to the parish beginning in 1870 because of cheap and plentiful farmland and initially planned to grow wheat, which the region's excessive rainfall made impossible. As a result, some of the German families who had settled in an area later named Roberts Cove began to experiment with rice. They incorporated an ox-driven thresher into rice cultivation, which separated grains of rice from the stalk and the chaff much more quickly than had been done by hand.

Shortly after, another wave of Germans set up farming operations near Rayne and introduced even more innovations, including new methods of manipulating water to control the flooding and draining of rice fields. Nicholas Zaunbrecher, whose descendants still farm rice in Acadia Parish today, is credited with inventing the modern rice pond in Louisiana, a knee-deep field surrounded by levees that could be flooded with water from a nearby reservoir.

Then in 1883, Iowa native and railroad agent Sylvester L. Cary recruited drought-weary, experienced midwestern wheat farmers to southwest Louisiana, where they adapted their gang plows, seeders, and disc harrows to rice cultivation. Cary became a founder of the town of Jennings. And in 1884, former Iowan Maurice Bryan revolutionized the industry by adapting an ox-driven twine binder to harvest rice.

Rice began to thrive in Acadia Parish not only because of these farming innovations but also because of the region's distinct geographical features. The parish is part of a flat, coastal prairie that stretches approximately from Lafayette into east Texas. The first eight to ten inches of soil in the prairie is topsoil, and underneath that is clay hardpan, which acts like a bowl and holds water in place when farmers flood their fields to encourage rice stubble to grow.

The rice industry developed further when a railroad line connected New Orleans to Houston and passed through the town of Crowley, which consequently became the Acadia Parish seat. Rice mills opened in Crowley that purchased "rough" rice (grains still covered by their outer hull) from farmers and processed it for commercial sale. And since water was such an important natural resource in rice cultivation, enterprising landowners in the area dug canals and sold access to them to their rice-farming neighbors.

In 1908, LSU opened the nation's first experimental rice research station in Rayne, a short distance east of Crowley, for the purpose of breeding varieties of rice that could thrive in Louisiana's climate, and also to help farmers troubleshoot diseases and pests. Throughout the twentieth century, the research station developed hundreds of new varieties that have been grown extensively throughout the South, including a variety of southern "jazzmen" rice, which mimics the flavor and texture of Asian jasmine rice.

Today, there are about 400,000 acres of land in rice production in Louisiana. The state is the third-largest rice producer in the United States; only Arkansas and California grow more. Louisiana rice farmers primarily grow long- and medium-grain rice, selling a large portion of their harvest to Kellogg's, Anheuser-Busch, and other major food and beverage companies, as well as to national rice labels. But some farmers sell their rice as a local, Louisiana-grown product under new farm-to-table labels.

Jackie Loewer, a former chairman of the USA Rice Federation, is a third-generation rice farmer whose grandfather immigrated to Roberts Cove in 1907. Today, he and his brother and nephew farm nearly three thousand acres of rice and soybeans around Rayne.

Jackie and I stand in front of one of his rice fields on a cool day in the early spring. The muddy swath of land is being graded by one of Jackie's workers, who drives back and forth in a tractor, smoothing out the wet earth so that rice seeds can be planted on an even surface. Jackie will seed his fields by air in March. Then he will flood the fields with water extracted from a deep well on his farm. He'll harvest the rice in August or September with large combines that efficiently push their way through the soggy fields thick with grassy stalks. There is no single way to grow rice, Jackie tells me. Some farmers distribute seeds by plane; others use on-the-ground equipment. Some plant in wet fields, others in dry.

Once the rice is harvested and separated, grains of rough rice are placed in large steel bins to dry. You can see them everywhere in this part of Louisiana, beacons sprouting from the flat landscape. The bins can hold up to 2,200 barrels—180 tons—of rough rice. Jackie reaches into a small door near the bottom of a bin and grabs a handful of grains, which he pours into my hand. They are light brown and still in their hard hulls. When the rice has dried to the proper level—12 percent moisture content is ideal—it's time to sell the crop to a mill.

Avenue D in downtown Crowley is the historic heart of Louisiana's rice milling industry; it was once home to fourteen rice mills. Changes in the industry, including consolidation and better technology, have reduced that number to two. The smaller of the operations is Falcon Rice, which has carved out a niche milling and packaging rice grown only in Louisiana. Its Cajun Country brand is sold in long grain, medium grain, jasmine rice, and popcorn rice—an aromatic rice similar to jasmine.

After a farmer arranges to sell his harvest to a rice mill, the rice is transported by truck from bin to mill. The trucks enter a weigh station at the mill, and the haul is weighed and its moisture level measured. It's hauled inside the complex and placed in another bin until time to mill it. During the milling process, the hull and bran are removed and sold for animal feed. The remaining "head" rice is then polished and packaged for human consumption.

Falcon's chief executive officer, Robbie Trahan, is a third-generation rice miller who grew up in Crowley and recently returned home with his wife and young children to take over the management of the family business. After graduating from the University of Louisiana at Lafayette, he spent years living and working as a certified public accountant in Houston and San Antonio. Opportunities for CPAs had been better in Texas than in Louisiana in the 1980s and 1990s, but he lamented leaving home.

Robbie and I discuss Crowley's International Rice Festival, founded in 1937 and one of the state's oldest and largest community celebrations, attracting tens of thousands of guests every October. Part of the festival is a cooking contest in which children and adults show how well they can cook various rice dishes.

We talk about the significance of rice in the home kitchens and restaurants of Louisiana. For a dish with very little flavor, its cooking process provokes strong opinions. "Rice is all about texture," Robbie says. "It makes a dish feel and taste a certain way in your mouth, and it's not the same when it's not prepared right."

A couple of years earlier, I witnessed how important rice is to the people of this region at an event at my son Christopher's school called "You Are What You Eat Day," part of a unit on the United States' history of immigration. Students were encouraged to bring foods representing their ethnic backgrounds. Tables outside the classroom held quiche, French cheeses, baguettes, Vietnamese pork wrapped in banana leaves, spaghetti and meatballs, Belgian waffles, and other dishes loosely tied to each child's heritage. As I was helping to arrange the table, my friend Celeste Dolan, a Crowley native, appeared with a lidded pot of something. It was cooked white rice still in Celeste's faithful rice pot, a common appliance in the town that steams rather than boils rice. "Hey, I'm from the Rice Capital of the World," she said. "We take it seriously."

Celeste later told me that stovetop rice pots, as well as electric rice cookers, were popular in Crowley when she was growing up because they cooked rice evenly. Both worked by the same premise. Rice and water were placed together in the main chamber, while water in a separate chamber below provided enough steam to cook the rice. No one in a town like Crowley wanted to be tripped up by something as important as rice, and a rice pot or rice cooker meant an even texture and no crunchy, burned bits of rice on the bottom of the pot. Indeed, Celeste's rice that day was perfectly steamed and the grains were full and plump but still beautifully loose.

Not everyone in these parts relies on a rice cooker. Steve Linscombe, head of LSU AgCenter's rice research station and a native of Gueydan (pronounced GAY-don), west of Crowley, insists that rice should be cooked in a lidded saucepan using slightly less water than the usual two-to-one ratio of water to rice. To the water he adds a little white vinegar. Ed Braud, one of Gonzales's most well-known outdoor jambalaya cooks, and his wife, Audrey, prepare rice on the stove the way most people cook pasta, by boiling it with the lid off until the rice has absorbed the water.

However tasty red beans and rice or shrimp Creole may be, they're ruined if rice is subpar. Commander's Palace chef Tory McPhail and owner Ti Adelaide Martin told me once in an interview for a food magazine how seriously rice is treated in the kitchen of the famed New Orleans restaurant. That station in the kitchen was one of the most important, they said. Across town in the Crescent City, Rayne native Isaac Toups, who founded the inventive Cajun restaurant Toups' Meatery, says that rice is a key dish on his meat-centric menu, and one that he's constantly monitoring—often tossing out inferior batches. Rice is no less a big deal for home cooks. Years ago, I was given the responsibility of preparing rice to go with my then-boyfriend's mother's crawfish étouffée. "You didn't salt the water, did you?" she asked matter-of-factly during dinner. "This tastes like it needs salt, and I know it's not my étouffée." Oops.

On Memorial Day weekend, my daughter Marien and I head for the Jambalaya Festival in the heart of Gonzales. Most of what we see on the grounds is the generic stuff of festivals all over the country: midway rides and basketball tosses erected and run by traveling carnies who were probably in Arkansas or Oklahoma last week, an antique-car show, and booths selling thong sandals and festival tchotchkes. Even the food trucks near the roller coasters and Ferris wheels are universal; they feature a prosaic mix of caramel apples, corndogs, and popcorn. But in a grassy field next to the Knights of Columbus hall, the first of several rounds of competition is underway in the jambalaya cook-off, which is about as authentic a food experience as it gets.

Twelve cooking teams are positioned side by side in an L-shape. All men in this round, each duo is dressed in matching shirts, often sporting the name of the small business sponsoring the team be it a day care center or an auto parts store. Many have competed before and are back to redeem themselves. They have practiced extensively during the year for friends and family, scribbling down notes about what worked and what didn't. And they have picked the brains of veteran cooks in the community for new strategies and advice on timing. Jambalaya is not the kind of dish that can be easily corrected if something goes wrong; you can't judge its flavor and texture until it's too late to turn back. The contestants know they have one shot to get it right.

Marien and I stand in the hot sun behind the barricade and watch as the teams tend their fires and chop vegetables. Many have come with manual industrial dicers to simplify the job of cutting large amounts of onions. One team's dicer is affixed to a homemade wooden frame that sits upright on a tabletop. A burly cook in a bright blue t-shirt slides an oversized peeled white onion into the dicer, pulls down on the crank, and uniform chunks spill into an aluminum bowl below.

The first round of competition requires teams to prepare thirty pounds of chicken and ten pounds of rice, but if they make it to the finals, they'll have to cook double that amount. We watch one team lower pieces of raw chicken into the hot oil; we are close enough to hear the meat sizzle and see the smoke begin to rise. Flames lick the bottom of the cast-iron pot. Each team has a paneled iron screen around their fire to keep it from spreading, and this screen features a cutout image of an LSU eye of the tiger, the same symbol that sit on the fifty-yard-line of Tiger Stadium. Elsewhere, another team is adding diced onions, bell peppers, and celery to their cauldron. Some teams cook these items separately; others cook them together with the chicken. Most will pour off the excess oil in grease containers before they add the rice, water, and seasonings.

As Marien and I watch, a woman approaches and asks us if we have anybody in the competition. The vast majority of the crowd is from the area, and they are there to root for brothers, uncles, husbands, and cousins. The woman, a longtime teacher in Ascension Parish named Angela Vercher, points to a few contestants and then to their relatives standing in the crowd. Many of the spectators are past winners. Hearing her talk about this person's cousin and that contestant's grandfather, it occurs to me that there may be fewer degrees of separation in Gonzales and its environs than anywhere else on earth.

As the minutes tick by, fire management becomes the contestants' biggest concern. We watch a team tamp down remaining flames and rake the coals to the periphery so they form a ring on the ground just outside the pot.

The cooks place lids on their pots but don't leave them unattended. Every so often, we watch them remove the lids and fold the rice over with long metal paddles, walking the circumference of the pot to make sure each section has been carefully turned and the pieces of chicken and aromatic vegetables are evenly distributed. Suddenly, one team expresses restrained frustration. Their fire has been too hot, and they unearth a swath of scorched rice from the bottom. It's a heartbreaking realization at this point in the competition.

At the end of the two-hour round, the cooks are bathed in sweat—they've been cooking over an open fire in ninety-degree heat. They ladle samples of their jambalaya into numbered Styrofoam containers and place them in ice chests that will be driven by flatbed trailer to the judges' stand for blind evaluation. Meanwhile, the jambalaya that remains in their pots is moved to the grandstand, where it can be purchased by festival goers. Some of it will be good, Angela Vercher tells Marien and me, and some not so much. The contestants are exhausted but hopeful. In a few minutes, the judges will announce the winner of this round. The lucky team will advance to the next round and later today will have to prepare perfect jambalaya all over again.

Chicken and Sausage Jambalaya

Edward Braud III is a past champion of the World Jambalaya Cook-off in Gonzales and one of Ascension Parish's famed outdoor cooks. He has been making Cajun jambalaya and scads of other dishes over hardwood fires since he was a child. Ed keeps more than sixty seasoned cast-iron pots, vessels that have helped him prepare everything from peach cobbler to shrimp and corn soup to his famed jambalaya. The colorful local legend recently recorded his recipes, as well as his original cowboy poetry, in a self-published cookbook called *Black Iron and Cajun Spice*.

When I interviewed Ed and his wife, Audrey, at their home in Ascension Parish, he joked that every once in a while you're forced to make jambalaya indoors. This happened most notably when Ed worked weekend shifts years ago as an operator at a local chemical plant. He attempted to prepare jambalaya for his fellow encamped workers, but the only equipment available was an electric stove. Like Julia Child and the one-eyed hotplate that launched her into PBS fame, Ed made do. This recipe has been modified from Ed's formula for indoor jambalaya.

Serves 6 to 8.

 1 pound bone-in, skin-on chicken thighs
 Salt and pepper for seasoning chicken
 2 tablespoons vegetable oil
 2 cups chopped yellow onions
 1 cup chopped green bell pepper
 ½ pound smoked pork sausage, sliced ½-inch thick
 2 cups raw long-grain white rice
 3 ½ cups water
 1 teaspoon salt
 ½ teaspoon black pepper
 ½ teaspoon cayenne pepper
 ½ teaspoon dried thyme
 2 bay leaves

Preheat oven to 350 degrees F. Season chicken liberally on both sides with salt and pepper. Using an oven-safe Dutch oven or large heavy pot, heat oil to medium-high and sauté chicken until each side is golden brown, about 4 minutes on each side. Remove pieces and set aside.

Add onions, bell pepper, and sausage to the pot and sauté until vegetables are soft and sausage is browned. Return chicken to the pot, and add rice, water, salt, black pepper, cayenne pepper, thyme, and bay leaves. Bring to a boil, then place in oven uncovered.

After 10 minutes, remove the pot and carefully fold the rice over, working each section of the pot once. Cover the pot, and return to the oven. Repeat the folding procedure every 10 minutes until the rice has thoroughly absorbed the liquid and the grains have "popped," about 45 minutes.

Creole Jambalaya with Shrimp and Andouille

In contrast to Cajun jambalaya, which gets its characteristic "paper bag" color from browned chicken, hen, or pork and smoked sausage, Creole-style jambalaya made in and around New Orleans is often prepared with shrimp and sometimes oysters. It gets its reddish hue from the addition of tomatoes, tomato sauce or tomato paste, a hallmark of Creole cuisine. This version, which I created for my seafood-and-spice-loving son, Christopher, is plenty rich and slightly smoky. Its use of both bacon and andouille sausage was inspired by some of the Creole jambalaya recipes of New Orleans chef John Besh. I prefer medium-grain rice in this dish because it absorbs liquid and flavor efficiently and pops with ease.

Serves 6.

> 6 ounces bacon, diced
> 6 ounces andouille sausage, diced
> 1 medium yellow onion, chopped
> 1 green bell pepper, chopped
> 1 red, orange, or yellow bell pepper, chopped
> 2 celery stalks with leaves, chopped
> 3 cloves garlic, minced
> 2 cups raw medium-grain rice
> 3 ½ cups chicken or shellfish stock
> ½ cup tomato sauce
> ½ teaspoon salt
> Several grinds fresh black pepper
> ⅛ teaspoon cayenne pepper or several dashes Tabasco sauce
> (omit if you like it mild)
> ½ teaspoon dried oregano
> 3 bay leaves
> 1 cup diced fresh tomatoes
> 1 ½ pounds large Gulf shrimp, peeled and deveined

2 tablespoons chopped green onions, green parts only

2 tablespoons chopped parsley

Cook bacon and andouille over medium heat in large Dutch oven for 3–5 minutes, or until fat is rendered and bacon is browned. Add onion, bell pepper, and celery. Sauté until soft, about 5 minutes. Add garlic and sauté 1–2 minutes.

Add rice, stock, tomato sauce, salt, black pepper, cayenne pepper, oregano, and bay leaves. Bring to a boil, then cover and reduce heat to low. Simmer for 10 minutes, then quickly fold over rice once to ensure it is not sticking to the bottom. Return lid to pot. After 10 more minutes, the liquid should be nearly absorbed, but the rice should still be loose and moist. Stir in tomatoes, shrimp, green onions, and parsley, blending well throughout the rice. Cook for another 3–5 minutes, or until the shrimp are just firm and pink.

3

The Curious Case of Creole Cream Cheese

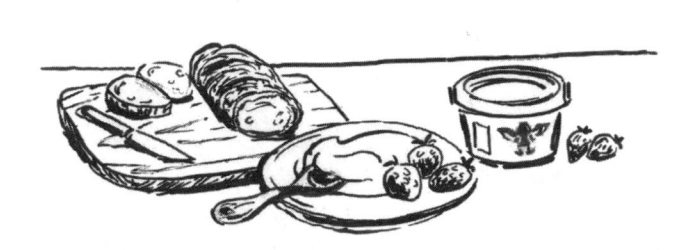

Early one June morning, on a day that promises to be a scorcher, fifth-generation dairy farmer Katie Mauthe Cutrer is busy arranging her vendor's booth at the Covington Farmers Market. The patrons have yet to arrive, and Katie and the other farmers and producers around her are getting ready, stacking piles of fresh summer produce, situating ice chests of brown shrimp from the Gulf of Mexico, and organizing fruit pies and jars of homemade jams and pickles. Katie has a cooler full of dairy products from her family's farm in McComb, Mississippi, including half-gallon glass bottles of cream-topped milk produced from a small herd of Jersey and Holstein cows that were milked the day before. She has also brought heavy cream, butter, plain yogurt, and tubs of a soft, farmstead cheese called Creole cream cheese. A mystery to some and a long-lost treasure to others, Creole cream cheese was once common in New Orleans and some parts of rural southern Louisiana. Now it's a rare find.

At 8 a.m., residents from Covington, a prosperous New Orleans bedroom community on the north shore of Lake Pontchartrain, begin streaming into the open-air market. Katie's patrons generally fall into one of two groups: mothers with young children who want small batch, homogenized milk produced from humanely treated cows, and older customers who are there specifically for the Mauthe's (pronounced MOH-tay) Creole cream cheese. For them, seeing it triggers a flood of nostalgia.

Few foods in Louisiana's gastronomic tableau are as divided by age, memory, and geography as Creole cream cheese, a mild, unripened cheese once made extensively in south Louisiana homes and by the bevy of family-owned local dairies that used to operate in and around New Orleans. With a soft, pliable texture akin to flan, Creole cream cheese was usually served in a bowl and topped with sugar and fresh fruit, or spread on toasted French bread and sprinkled with salt and cracked black pepper. For Catholics who abstained from meat on Fridays, it was a common end-of-week breakfast staple.

I learned about Creole cream cheese when I covered its comeback for several publications in the late 1990s, about the same time that farmers markets and artisanal food production were gaining traction in Louisiana. Until then, I had never heard of Creole cream cheese. It wasn't because I didn't grow up here. There were plenty of native Louisianans who were also unaware of it. In fact, most people I mentioned Creole cream cheese to in Baton Rouge hadn't been exposed to it. Knowledge of it was largely confined to those with roots in New Orleans and certain Cajun communities.

In New Orleans, Creole cream cheese was once sold by street vendors, many of them Creole women who peddled the dish from carts around the city throughout the nineteenth century. By the early twentieth century, Creole cream cheese was wildly popular in New Orleans, and local dairies began selling it to their customers. Milkmen delivered the fresh cheese along with bottles of milk. Plenty of families both in the city and the country also prepared it themselves, by letting raw milk sour and thicken naturally. Because of its gentle flavor and soft consistency, it was a food consumed by the young, the infirm, and the elderly, bolstering the sentimentality surrounding it. Creole cream cheese wasn't particularly versatile nor was its flavor assertive, but it was a comforting, appealing food associated with nurture and care.

Its demise, therefore, was a big deal to its enthusiasts. By the 1980s, Creole cream cheese had all but disappeared, a consequence of several factors that converged in the second half of the twentieth century, including tighter government regulations, economic changes impacting smaller, regional dairies, and domestic cooking habits. But in 1999, a native New Orleanian named Poppy Tooker decided it was time to save Creole cream cheese. Poppy, a well-known culinary instructor, author, and media personality, lamented the loss of the dish and began a one-woman crusade to teach people how to make it.

The possibility of a Creole cream cheese resurgence caused a profound reaction among the dish's aficionados, and the movement caught the attention of food journalists. At the time, Poppy was also involved in establishing a New Orleans chapter of Slow Food, the international organization whose mission then was to call attention to endangered indigenous food traditions. Slow Food was the perfect context in which to discuss the loss of Creole cream cheese as well as other endangered Louisiana dishes, including a sweet rice fritter called calas that was also sold by nineteenth-century New Orleans street vendors. But Poppy's effort to save Creole cream cheese garnered particular enthusiasm because a passionate group of people in south Louisiana remembered eating it in the sixties and seventies. Moreover, the dish captured the imagination of a new generation of local-foods followers who were patronizing new farmers markets in places like New Orleans, Baton Rouge, Covington, and Lafayette. At the same time, a handful of artisan dairy farmers, including Katie's father, Kenny Mauthe, saw an opportunity to manufacture Creole cream cheese. Kenny was already selling milk directly to consumers at the Crescent City Farmers Market, and he was confident that Creole cream cheese would also be well received. It seemed the stars had aligned for a Creole cream cheese comeback. But as he and others would later attest, resuscitating a nostalgia food was more complicated and challenging than it first appeared.

Creole cream cheese is so named because the dish was originally an Old World product made by French and German immigrants to Louisiana.

They produced unripened cheese by leaving raw milk to turn thick and chunky by its own natural lactic fermentation, creating a substance later called clabber in the American South. When the substance drained overnight, it formed a soft cheese that could be enhanced with salt or herbs, eaten on its own, topped with cream, or incorporated into other dishes. The culinary tradition stemmed from farmhouse thrift; there was no need to toss out leftover milk when you could convert it into another useful food.

In *New Orleans Cuisine: Fourteen Signature Dishes and Their Histories,* food historian Cynthia LeJeune Nobles pieces together the likely history of Creole cream cheese. She suggests it began with early eighteenth-century French colonists, who arrived in Louisiana with domestic cheese-making skills. Immigrants from Germany and France who settled in and around New Orleans established a robust dairy culture, raising dairy and beef cows and selling both meat and milk in the city's open air markets. In the Acadiana parishes west of Baton Rouge and New Orleans, where dairy farms were common, a version of the cheese also took root. Cajun and German families there would drain clabber and add cream, referring to it as cream clabber, cream cheese, or Creole cream cheese.

According to Nobles, by the early 1900s about 160 family-owned dairies functioned in the New Orleans area. Kenny Mauthe's grandparents' dairies were among them. The family of Henry Mauthe, Kenny's father, had dairied in the Alsace-Lorraine region of France and had immigrated to New Orleans in the late nineteenth century. The family established a dairy near the city's Industrial Canal area. Kenny's mother's family also had a dairy, located in the Gentilly section of New Orleans. Both sides of the family made Creole cream cheese. Later, the Mauthe Family Dairy, run by Henry Mauthe, was one of several local dairies that made and sold Creole cream cheese in New Orleans in the middle of the twentieth century.

By then, larger commercial dairies in New Orleans—including Borden's, Brown's Velvet, Roemer's, and Gold Seal—routinely made Creole cream cheese, along with milk, butter, cream, and other dairy products, and delivered them to local residences. The commercial availability of

Creole cream cheese helped make it a regular part of life and secured its place on family menus. But the ease with which New Orleanians could buy Creole cream cheese had an unfortunate side effect. People stopped making it at home.

The first half of the twentieth century was the peak of Creole cream cheese in Louisiana. But as the family dairy business began to change, so did the availability of the product. Milk prices stagnated in the 1970s, and many smaller, local dairies—frustrated by what they were earning for raw milk—sold out to national conglomerates. At the same time, the U.S. Department of Agriculture (USDA) introduced new regulations prohibiting the production of milk and other dairy products, including cheese, in the same plant. Consequently, many local dairies stopped producing Creole cream cheese by the mid-1980s. To make matters worse, the USDA also banned the sale of raw milk, making it nearly impossible for home-based Creole cream cheese makers to prepare it in the traditional fashion. (States were allowed to adopt their own raw milk policies. As of early 2014, Louisiana had maintained a prohibition on raw milk sales to consumers.)

By the late 1980s, the dairy world in New Orleans was a pale imitation of its former self, with no home deliveries, few local dairies, and virtually no commercial Creole cream cheese. But what particularly bothered Poppy, a spirited local-foods advocate who uses the tagline "Eat it to save it," was that knowledge of how to prepare Creole cream cheese had nearly vanished. She began her movement to resurrect Creole cream cheese by demonstrating how easy it was to make it at home.

Early in her crusade, Poppy acquired a recipe for Creole cream cheese from the Centanni family, who had owned the local Gold Seal Dairy. The company had made one of the most popular commercial versions of the dish. Poppy modified the recipe for everyday use and began demonstrating how to make it. Since the late 1990s, she has given countless Creole cream cheese lessons, but she still recalls the crowd that gathered on Saturday, August 28, 1999, when she pulled out her recipe, equipment, and finished product at the Crescent City Farmers Market.

August is normally a slow time for south Louisiana farmers markets. It's ghastly hot, and the summer crops that have borne fruit since May are nearly depleted. The sun is intense, even early in the morning, and the air is moist and heavy. Still, a record number of market goers surrounded Poppy's booth that day to learn how to restore the traditional dish to their kitchens.

Poppy, known for her wit and unrelenting loyalty to New Orleans, chirped about the recipe's ease, holding up her personal collection of cheese molds—recycled round plastic food containers. Into the sides and bottoms of each she had poked a dozen or so small holes with a soldering iron. The preparation of Creole cream cheese, she said, involved nothing more than combining skim milk, buttermilk, rennet, and salt in a large aluminum bowl and letting it sit out on the counter at room temperature for twenty-four hours. She laughed in the face of the food safety implications, delivering a line she's used frequently since: "You say to the average person around the country that you're going to take a dairy product and let it sit out for a day, and they look at you like you're crazy. It's a clear illustration of how passionate we feel about our local foods down here."

The rest of the recipe is simple. As the cheese sits overnight, the rennet, a natural coagulating agent, causes the liquid whey to pull away from the solid clabber, leaving a large, soft, single curd. To complete the recipe, you simply scoop out hunks of the curd with a slotted spoon and ladle each spoonful into one of the cheese molds. Place the molds onto rimmed baking sheets, cover them with plastic wrap, and put them in the refrigerator. Over the next several hours, the whey continues to drain through the container holes and onto the baking sheets, after which the Creole cream cheese is slightly firm, deliciously tart, and ready to consume.

On that same steamy August morning, Henry and Kenny Mauthe, vendors at the market, noticed the commotion outside Poppy's demonstration, and the wheels began to turn. Henry Mauthe had long since moved his dairy operation out of New Orleans fifty miles north to Folsom, Louisiana, but he still remembered making and selling Creole cream cheese at the old family dairy, and how well received it had been by local consumers. He and Kenny believed that by selling the product directly to consumers at the Crescent City Farmers Market, Creole cream cheese could once again be a successful commercial venture.

The Mauthes reached out to Poppy, and they began the process of researching what it would take to produce the cheese at Henry's farm. They worked for a year with state dairy inspectors to install the proper equipment. To perfect the recipe, the Mauthes experimented with Tooker and former LSU AgCenter dairy science professor Ronald Gough to develop a large-scale formula that could produce Creole cream cheese with the taste and consistency fans would remember. Meanwhile, Henry Mauthe was approached by a man who had gotten wind of the family's plans. Somewhere along the way, the man had picked up about a thousand hard plastic twelve-ounce Creole cream cheese molds from Borden's defunct production line. The elder Mauthe traded an antique double-barrel shotgun for the molds, and another piece of the production puzzle fell into place.

The Mauthes' Creole cream cheese–making operation was well on its way by 2001. Kenny Mauthe brought samples of his product to a small group gathered at Poppy's house that included *New Orleans Times-Picayune* restaurant critic and feature writer Brett Anderson and former *Times-Picayune* columnist Lolis Eric Elie, who both praised its quality. In July 2001, Anderson wrote an article in the paper announcing the return of the beloved dish at the Mauthe booth at the Crescent City Farmers Market the following Tuesday. By the time the Mauthes arrived that morning, a line had formed that soon stretched around the block. Kenny's wife Jamie sold more than five hundred containers of Creole cream cheese—everything she had brought to the market—within forty-five minutes.

The hubbub notwithstanding, it was actually still possible to find Creole cream cheese commercially. A popular independent grocery store in nearby Metairie, Dorignac's Food Center, had begun making a version in 1986 that is still prepared daily. But the process included heating the skim milk, buttermilk, and rennet, and purists like Poppy found the product inauthentic. Dorignac's Creole cream cheese still maintains a strong following, but the Mauthes had accomplished something noteworthy: They had revived a near-extinct dish through the purview of the local-foods movement. Mauthe's Creole cream cheese wasn't just a re-release. It was a farmstead cheese made in small batches with minimally processed milk from a herd of well-tended, sweet-faced Jersey and Holstein cows.

The Mauthes weren't the only ones to spot the opportunity to revive the dish. At the time that they and Poppy were effectively joining forces, John Folse, an internationally recognized chef and a champion of Louisiana culinary traditions, was on the verge of launching an artisanal dairy at his Bittersweet Plantation. A successful restaurateur, caterer, and food manufacturer based in Gonzales, Louisiana, Folse began producing boutique cheeses, butter, Bulgarian yogurt, and Creole cream cheese, which he had grown up eating in St. James Parish, southwest of New Orleans. And Smith Creamery, a family-owned dairy in the piney woods region west of Baton Rouge, also began manufacturing Creole cream cheese. The Smiths had been selling their farmstead milk and butter at the Crescent City Farmers Market and the Red Stick Farmers Market in Baton Rouge, but when they saw the new enthusiasm for Creole cream cheese, they spent months developing their own recipe, giving out samples to customers familiar with the product to see how their version fared.

In the early 2000s, it seemed Creole cream cheese was finally on stable ground in New Orleans and Baton Rouge, with a small but devoted handful of producers keeping it alive and a growing number of local-foods patrons snapping it up in specialty grocery stores and farmers markets. Then things changed again. The fragile return of Creole cream cheese was disrupted by a series of unrelated events.

Hurricane Katrina was the first. The massive August 2005 storm caused a breach in the New Orleans levee system, resulting in the flooding of 80 percent of the city and its surrounding areas. Nearly nineteen hundred people died and the region suffered billions in damage. Thousands of residents were forced to leave their homes for months; some never returned. The impact of Hurricane Katrina was felt by every strata of society and every social and economic institution in New Orleans, including the Crescent City Farmers Market.

Henry's farm in Folsom and Kenny and Jamie's farm in McComb, Mississippi, were spared serious damage. But their customers at the time were exclusively in New Orleans. The Mauthes had sold up to fourteen hundred tubs of Creole cream cheese a week at farmers markets and grocery stores in the city. With those outlets shuttered and their patrons scattered—some for months and even years after the storm—the Mauthes' business came to an abrupt halt.

Money tight, Kenny and Jamie suspended operations and took jobs outside of farming. He worked for a refinery, and she took a position at a flower shop. They sold off their cows and all but about fifty acres of their original 335-acre tract. The break from dairying gave them a chance to get back on solid financial footing, but the pull of the industry was powerful. A few years after the storm, Kenny and Jamie started the slow, uphill climb to rebuild their operations, moving the cheese-making function to their farm, which they renamed Progress Milk Barn. They acquired a few cows at a time and began to sell milk at farmers markets in Mississippi. It would take them six years to resume full production of milk and Creole cream cheese.

Theirs wasn't the only tragedy felt among Creole cream cheese manufacturers. In the summer of 2011, a leaking propane tank exploded at Smith Creamery in Mount Hermon, causing irreparable damage to the dairy. Smith Creamery was eventually bought by a large regional dairy, Kleinpeter Farms, and resumed its small-batch milk operations. But it discontinued making Creole cream cheese.

Another pivotal event occurred in 2012, when John Folse decided to close his Bittersweet Plantation Dairy to spend time on other projects. The chef's food manufacturing business was growing substantially, and he had formed a restaurant development company that had just opened a new upscale eatery, R'evolution, in New Orleans.

Smith Creamery and Bittersweet Plantation Dairy were exiting the Creole cream cheese business at the same time that Kenny and Jamie Mauthe were finding their way back into it. By late 2012, the Mauthes were juggling four farmers markets, several grocery stores, and a handful of restaurants. They had rebuilt their herd as well—and they were routinely selling out of their products.

‿∂‿

Dairy cows set a specific, unflinching rhythm on a farm. They must be milked twice a day to ensure their milk flows at its highest and healthiest levels. The Mauthes don't push production with hormones; they let their cows meander and eat grass growing on the Mississippi farm's rolling pastureland. The cows dutifully wander toward the barn every day at 5 a.m. and 5 p.m. to be milked.

Early on a Monday morning in the fall, Kenny and Katie are making Creole cream cheese, while Jamie and the Mauthes' other grown daughter, Sara, are using it to make homemade cheesecakes in a separate commercial kitchen on site. About one-third of the milk processed on the farm is used to make Creole cream cheese, and the balance goes into plain yogurt, some hard cheeses, mozzarella, butter, and milk.

The milk barn smells grassy and sweet. After the cows are milked, their fresh milk is pumped first into a cold tank and then into a fifty-gallon pasteurizer in the production room. After being pasteurized, the milk is piped into a small separator. The separator spins at a high speed, and its centrifugal force separates the cream from the milk, throwing each one into a different collecting vessel. To begin the Creole cream cheese-making process, Katie takes the milk and pours it into an open cylindrical tank. Then she adds enzymes that will separate the solid curds from the liquid whey overnight.

When that process is complete, as it is on this particular brisk, cloudy morning, Katie uses a plastic pitcher to remove the pale golden whey from the tank, disposing it in a work sink. When most of the liquid has been removed, she scoops up the pillowy cheese curds left behind in the tank with slotted twelve-ounce containers—the same ones for which her grandfather traded a vintage shotgun. Dressed in jeans, rubber boots, and a pink sweatshirt shirt and ball cap, she works methodically, her nimble fingers filling the molds and arranging them on rimmed plastic trays with corner holes that allow for drainage. When the trays are filled, she slides them onto racks on a rolling cart. The remaining whey continues to drain from each of the filled containers, dribbling down through tray holes onto the production room floor. The drip is soothing white noise, gentle and steady. After resting for half a day or more, the cheese will be ready to package and take to farmers markets or retail stores. Katie fills about 250 containers up to three times a week.

Each time I visited the Mauthes, who live about three hours round-trip from my home in Baton Rouge, I returned with as many tubs of their Creole cream cheese as my family and I could eat before their perishable date. I had long since fallen in love with the stuff, which was currently unavailable in Baton Rouge. The Mauthes' version of Creole cream cheese is something special—semi-tart, creamy, and rich, a consequence of the high butterfat content of the milk from the ir-resistibly cute, floppy-eared Jersey cows that roam their land, hesitantly but curiously checking out strangers like me. Every morning for a week after my research trips, we had Progress Milk Barn Creole cream cheese for breakfast, topped with fresh fruit and a little sugar. Our children especially loved its welcoming consistency and rich taste. No wonder so many people remember it fondly.

Kenny says he is encouraged by what seems to be a rising demand for Creole cream cheese, buoyed by the local-foods movement. "We're at that point where we need to expand," he says. He wears a hat from Lüke, an Alsatian-style brasserie in New Orleans and San Antonio founded by Chef John Besh. A New Orleans restaurateur who opened a wave of eateries in post-Katrina New Orleans, Besh has made a point to tap Louisiana producers for many of his ingredients. After the storm, the

John Besh Foundation gave Kenny and Jamie a $20,000 loan to help install new equipment to establish cheese-making operations on their farm in Mississippi, and the chef has bought many of their products.

Still, it isn't easy to make a living in the dairy world. Many artisan producers in the South have a hard time charging the same prices seen in other parts of the United States where boutique foods have been more extensively embraced. The overhead associated with each bottle of milk or container of Creole cream cheese can be exorbitant, keeping the Mauthes' profit margins exceptionally low. And though demand for their products now exceeds supply, the family must carefully consider how to expand their herd and production cycle without overextending themselves.

Katie never wanted a career in anything other than dairying. She fills the last container of Creole cream cheese deftly and washes down the prep sink, ready for the next chore. There is no shortage of them. Every day is spent either preparing for or manning the farmers markets in Louisiana and Mississippi. In between, she milks the cows, keeps up equipment, and tends her own family.

The closest interstate highway to the Mauthes' land is more than twenty miles away, and the main road leading to it is buffered by trees and hills. The farm is calm and peaceful. A breeze whips through stately water oaks and scrub brush in the pasture.

Kenny looks out at the cows. Like Creole cream cheese itself, he occupies a tiny subset of the American culinary world struggling for sustainability. It's where he wants to be. "Being a dairy farmer is all I've ever known," he says. "All I've ever done."

Creole Cream Cheese

Creole cream cheese has been most commonly eaten topped with sugar and fresh fruit or else sprinkled with cracked black pepper and spread on toast. But if you're lucky enough to get hold of a tub or ambitious enough to make it yourself, you'll discover a range of uses. The Mauthe family incorporates it in homemade cheesecakes and tosses it in a skillet with butter to make cream sauce for pasta. Because the cheese is tart and sturdy, it makes a decadent baked potato topper. It can also be combined with milk, cream, sugar, and vanilla extract and frozen to make frozen Creole cream cheese, one of its most popular offshoots. But first, you have to try your hand at the master recipe, and Poppy Tooker's version is the best place to start.

Makes approximately 16 cups (8 molded pints).

> 1 gallon skim milk
> 1 cup buttermilk
> 6 to 8 drops liquid vegetable rennet (available in health food
>   stores)
> Pinch of salt
> 8 pint-size cheese molds (see note)

In a large stainless steel or glass bowl, combine skim milk, buttermilk, rennet, and salt. Cover lightly with plastic wrap and leave out on a kitchen counter at room temperature for 18 to 24 hours. You will then find one large cheese curd floating in whey. Use a slotted spoon to fill molds with the cheese, placing each one on a tray rack in a roasting pan so it can continue to drain. Cover lightly with plastic wrap. Discard the remaining whey in the bowl. Refrigerate for 6 to 8 hours. Turn cheese out of molds and store in tightly covered containers for up to two weeks.

Note: You can make your own cheese molds by using a soldering iron to poke holes in plastic pint containers.

Recipe courtesy of Poppy Tooker.

Creole Cream Cheese Banana Bread with
Cranberries and Pistachios

My family has always enjoyed a warm slice of breakfast bread, and
when I'm lucky enough to have a little extra Creole cream cheese lying
around, I add it to my basic banana bread formula. It provides a tangy
note and adds a layer of richness.

Makes 1 loaf.

    2 cups self-rising flour
    ½ teaspoon baking soda
    ½ teaspoon salt
    1 teaspoon cinnamon
    1 cup tightly packed brown sugar
    ¼ cup canola oil
    ½ cup Creole cream cheese or Greek yogurt (full fat is best, but
        low or no-fat will do)
    3 very ripe bananas, mashed
    2 large eggs
    1 teaspoon vanilla extract
    ¼ cup dried cranberries
    ¼ cup chopped pistachios, walnuts or pecans

Preheat oven to 350 degrees F. In a medium bowl, combine flour, baking soda, salt, and cinnamon. In another bowl, whisk sugar, oil, and
Creole cream cheese until well combined. Add bananas, eggs one at a
time, and vanilla. Add flour mixture slowly to wet batter. Stir until well
combined. Do not overmix. Fold in cranberries and pistachios. Pour
into a greased and lightly floured 8x4-inch loaf pan and bake for 1 hour.
Cool for about 10 minutes. Remove loaf from pan and let continue to
cool on a wire rack for 10 more minutes.

4

Summer Snow
Snoballs

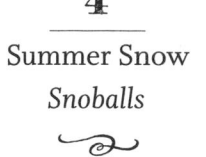

Ashley Hansen is looking for the *good ice.*

She lifts the lid of one chest freezer after another until she finds a block that has the cloudy opalescence and slick surface that comes with the right amount of cold and time. Ice that has just been delivered to her family's snoball stand seems like it would be cold enough, but the sweltering July heat outside has softened its surface. And a block buried deep in one of the freezers is too hard and dry. She is looking for ice that falls somewhere in the middle. She'll know it when she sees it.

"It's hard to describe," she says, running her petite, tanned hands over a block's chilly face, reading its veins and fissures for signs of how it will behave. She wants a block that will yield to the whirring blades of her grandfather's ice-shaving machine and neatly transform into a substance that looks and feels like real snow.

She spots one, eases it out of its clear plastic package, and slides it into the opening of the countertop machine here at Hansen's Sno-Bliz in uptown New Orleans, the iconic snoball stand founded in the 1930s by her grandparents Ernest and Mary Hansen. She presses a sandaled foot onto a floor pedal to wake up the machine, a cylindrical drum footed on four thin steel rods. The pedal sets in motion a trio of circular blades inside the cavity. Her left hand works a lever that guides the ice toward its fate, while her right hand waits underneath for a shower of shavings to fall from a hidden chute.

She feels the consistency of the ice and lets it drop into the pan below. The flurries feel too wet, too matted together. The machine, like everything else on this summer day, is hot. But within a minute or two, the block cools the steel down, and the machine begins to churn out shaved ice with the soft, pillowy texture she expects.

Ashley fills a paper cup halfway with the flurries, picks up an unlabeled glass bottle fitted with a diffuser, and pours sweet syrup the shade of pink cotton candy over the ice, rotating the cup for a thorough drenching. The shaved ice is so fine it takes a moment for the syrup to soak through completely. Another layer of snow comes next, enough to create an Everest-like peak on top, which gets its own dousing of pink liquid. Finally, she inserts the requisite duo of spoon and straw into the mound, completing the construction of an authentic New Orleans nectar cream snoball.

Nectar is a classic snoball flavor beloved by New Orleanians that has been around in the Crescent City as long as snoballs themselves. Local nectar recipes, Ashley tells me, are like recipes for gumbo or jambalaya. Everyone's grandmother had one, and hers was better than yours. Nectar is prepared by combining vanilla and almond extracts with simple syrup and a few dribbles of red food coloring. It is a flavor tied not only to New Orleans's snoball history, but to the history of the city's soda fountains. K&B Pharmacies, Schweickhardt Drugs, and others sold nectar sodas by the gross, made with electric red-pink syrup, soda water, and vanilla ice cream. Similarly, snoball stands served nectar and nectar cream snoballs; the latter was achieved by adding milk or cream to the syrup. Over the course of Hansen's long existence, the shop has served plenty of the creamy pink snoballs, and scads of other traditional flavors and toppings. Ashley and other modern snoball-stand operators have also branched out and crafted new small-batch flavors with natural extracts. She reaches for homemade cardamom syrup to flavor a second snoball for us, ginger syrup for a third, and two different syrups—satsuma and vanilla bean—for a final "half-and-half," with equal doses poured into the sides of the paper cup.

She puts the snoballs onto a tray and we head outside to a backless wooden bench facing the street. I'm secretly thrilled to be eating a snoball with Ashley. Quiet and contemplative, she is snoball royalty in a city that claims and exalts this distinctive summer treat. Locals have been coming to her family's stand for more than eighty years.

The snoballs served in New Orleans, and in some other parts of Louisiana, are a far cry from the snow cones I grew up eating in Georgia—jumbles of hard ice pebbles piled in white paper cones and drenched in primary colors. They were cool and sweet and they served their purpose, but here in my adopted state the ice is as soft as goose down and the flavors are endless and exotic.

The blanket of early afternoon heat bears down on Ashley and me, so we dive into the snoballs she's prepared. The cardamom is perfumey, and the ginger, peppery and sweet. In the half-and-half, the satsuma tastes sharp and citrusy, a refreshing foil to the creamy vanilla bean. We use the spoons to sample several bites of each one, including the mild, sweet nectar cream, which tastes the way a good bakery smells, like vanilla and almond. As the snoballs begin to melt under the punishing temperature, we use the straws to slurp up the leavings.

Hansen's is referred to as a "stand" in New Orleans snoball nomenclature, but it is actually a cinderblock building at the corner of Tchoupitoulas and Bordeaux Streets in uptown New Orleans. Whitewashed and trimmed in magenta, the place wears the patina of age and use. A simple sign with block lettering reads "Hansen's Sno-Bliz 1PM 7PM." New Orleanians know, however, that this means only during snoball season—an inexact period spanning mid-spring to early fall. The sign is hung above whiny screened doors through which families have passed for generations.

Shaved-ice confections are common in various forms in the United States and across the globe, but in New Orleans, they are an obsession and a rite of summer. The city is home to legacy stands like Hansen's, Williams Plum Street, and dozens of other neighborhood spots where adults and children return predictably to savor their favorite snoball flavors every year. Stands reopen in the springtime when the weather is warm enough to pique a craving for something sweet and cold. In New Orleans, that usually means after Fat Tuesday and the conclusion of Carnival. Stands come not only in the form of permanent buildings like Hansen's but also as mobile trailers, tumbledown attachments to buildings, and frame structures with just enough square footage to accommodate a worker, a mechanical ice shaver, a chest freezer, and an arrangement of syrups, toppings, and cups. The return of a stand in Louisiana might be announced simply with a hand-painted image of a snoball on a wordless wooden placard propped on the side of a rural road or city street, beckoning to passersby who understand the tradition.

Whether cramped or relatively roomy, somewhere in the configuration of the snoball stand is an unsophisticated sign with a list of available flavors. Empty cups with corresponding prices scribbled in Sharpie marker are often tacked to the wall, along with an assortment of handwritten messages to customers the management has found necessary to add over the years. At Williams Plum Street, a note reminds customers to provide the size of their order first—not the flavor—so the proprietor can get about the business of shaving enough ice to fill the correct vessel. Break this rule and get a stern warning. At Hansen's, the messages on the walls are so overwhelming that a banner requesting "Please Read This Sign" has been installed over the main list of flavors and toppings, an attempt to focus the overstimulated eye.

Indeed, it takes awareness and concentration to order an authentic snoball. There are several sizes and a dizzying number of flavors, from straightforward strawberry or bubblegum to insider favorites such as king cake, bananas Foster, frozen mint, Tiger's Blood (berry and coconut), and Brown Pelican (cream and root beer). In typical Louisiana fashion, snoballs can be made further decadent with the addition of condensed milk, crushed fruit, whipped cream, and ice cream. Snoball fans are usually partisan about their favorite flavors, and they tend to order them repeatedly.

Snoballs were first served in New Orleans by street vendors who rolled carts holding block ice they shaved with small hand planers. The confection's earliest form inspired Ashley's grandfather, Ernest Hansen, a machinist who had been educated at the Isaac Delgado Central Trades School (the forebear of Delgado Community College). When his son asked him for shaved ice from a mobile cart, Hansen wondered if there was a more efficient and sanitary way to produce it.

By then, ice-crushing machines had been invented. Dallas resident Albert Bert patented one of the first automated ice crushers in 1920, the year after he reportedly introduced the first snow cone at the Texas State Fair. But Hansen had ideas about how to improve machines that were already on the market. He built his first prototype in 1934 and completed a second in 1939, making enough substantive changes to the existing designs to earn a U.S. patent. His wife, Mary, the daughter of an Italian grocer, was confident in her ability to sell snoballs made with her husband's new "Sno-Bliz" machine, so she opened a stand on the sidewalk in front of her parents' home on St. Ann Street, selling the confection for two cents each, a penny higher than the going rate in New Orleans at the time.

The stand was a success, and the couple expanded their business briefly to Valmont Street, then to a dedicated corner store on Tchoupitoulas Street in 1944. It remains there today. Loyal patrons convinced that Ernest Hansen's hand-built machine still makes the fluffiest ice in town dutifully position themselves on a yellow floor stripe meant to keep the line orderly.

At the same time that Ernest and Mary Hansen were raising the bar on snoballs in New Orleans, a local grocer of Sicilian descent named George Ortolano was inventing another version of the ice-shaving machine that also produced cottony, shaved ice. Ortolano saw snoballs as a way to increase business at his corner grocery at Magazine and Delachaise streets during the Great Depression. By 1936, he had designed and built his own machine and installed it at his grocery store.

Snoballs were wildly popular among Ortolano's customers—they were cheap and helped ease the stifling temperatures. The grocer recognized he was onto something big. A handful of his relatives also owned grocery stores in town, and Ortolano made snoball machines for them, too, keenly aware that better availability of the product would expand awareness and sales. Early snoball operators like the Ortolanos and the Hansens, and Williams Plum Street Snoball founder Sydney Williams developed homemade flavors that sprang from ingredients common in grocery stores, including chocolate syrup, vanilla and almond extracts, and condensed milk, as well as added food coloring.

During World War II, Ortolano took a break from the grocery business to work in local shipyards to support the war effort. When he returned to business after the war, he focused exclusively on distributing his snoball machines. Hansen, in contrast, had little interest in replicating and commercializing his equipment. In fact, the few he sold to other vendors in New Orleans, he eventually bought back, expressing concerns about safety.

Ortolano perfected his design, adding galvanized metal and later stainless steel to make the machines stronger. He named his brainchild the SnoWizard "*SnoBall*" Machine. The name stuck. The icy confections have been referred to as snoballs in New Orleans ever since—and by extension, in much of Louisiana.

By then, budding entrepreneurs were considering entering the snoball business, and Ortolano—a master marketer—was happy to sell them the equipment. His brother Frank also played a role in expanding New Orleans's emergent snoball culture, designing a temporary wooden structure that was simple to set up in the spring and disassemble and store in the fall. Enterprising locals eager to augment their family incomes could open a stand quickly and at relatively little cost. SnoWizard continued to grow. Between the 1930s and 1970s, it was the principal

New Orleans–based commercial vendor of snoball machines, helping the culture spread within the city, as well as to other parts of Louisiana—including Shreveport, 330 miles to the northwest, clear on the other side of the state.

There, in the late 1960s, a manufacturing executive named Virgil Moseley dreamed of opening his own snoball stand. The confection was unheard-of then in Shreveport, but Moseley had discovered it as a child while visiting New Orleans with his older sister.

"Tasting those snoballs in New Orleans made a big impression on my dad," says Victoria Moseley Bayless, Moseley's daughter and curator of the Louisiana State University Arthropod Museum. "He loved the idea of making and selling snoballs," she added. "He kept it in the back of his mind that one day he would get into the business."

In 1969, Moseley took the plunge and contacted Ortolano about purchasing a SnoWizard ice-shaving machine. Since few north Louisianans knew of the New Orleans snoball tradition, the Moseleys presented the confection under an original name, "Alaska Delight," inspired by a family trip the year before along the Alaska Highway. They built a wooden trailer painted with murals depicting snowy scenes of animals and Native American tribes and mounted a totem pole on top. In 1970, Moseley, his wife, and their two teenage daughters hauled the trailer to the State Fair of Louisiana in Shreveport and began selling the first Alaska Delights.

In keeping with the Yukon theme, fifteen-year-old Victoria and her seventeen-year-old sister, Marlene, dressed in fur-trimmed parkas and gave out free samples to the crowd. Their unwitting patrons didn't know what to make of the shaved ice treats at first, but were soon were convinced. The consistency of the ice and the variety of the toppings were unlike anything they'd tasted before.

Alaska Delight developed a strong following in Shreveport throughout the 1970s. The Moseleys built a syrup kitchen onto their house and made homemade syrups to fit the motif, including Moose Milk, a vanilla flavor, and Gold Nugget, vanilla with coconut. Over the years, Moseley and Ortolano developed a close working relationship. The inventor took the entrepreneur under his wing, coaching him about the importance of the ice temperature, the condition of the blades, and the quality of ingredients. Ortolano believed that while snoballs were a simple product, their success rested on high standards. That meant using enough sugar in the simple syrup, even when sugar prices fluctuated wildly as they did in the 1970s.

Today, ice houses in Louisiana make standard, rectangular blocks of ice to slide into the multitudes of commercial snoball machines around the state. (Hansen's is an exception, requiring a slightly different size block.) But when the Moseleys were in business, they hand-trimmed their ice. Victoria learned to score and cut large blocks into perfect twelve-pound rectangles because the correct size and shape of the ice, along with its temperature, were essential in producing fluffy shavings. The family understood that the machine's blades would dull if the ice was too cold, so they developed a homespun system for making sure a block was ready. After taking it out of the freezer, they would place it in an ice chest for about two hours. If the ice was white on the ends, it was too cold; if it was too clear, it was too soft and it went back in to the freezer. The goal was somewhere in the middle.

The Moseleys eventually opened three permanent locations in Shreveport and a fourth in nearby Bossier City. They closed their stands in 1975 because of the high cost of sugar, but they continued the business on a smaller scale from their Alaska Delight trailer for several years after, serving snoballs at the State Fair in Shreveport and other festivals in north Louisiana until 2000.

❧

By the end of the twentieth century, snoballs had become fairly commonplace throughout Louisiana and in other parts of the Gulf South, thanks to the availability of commercial machines from companies like

SnoWizard and Southern Snow, another New Orleans–based vendor. Today, the SnoWizard business is run by Ortolano's nephew, Ronnie Sciortino, a former chef with an eye for detail who once worked at now-closed New Orleans legacy restaurants LeRuth's and Stephen & Martin.

In the early 1980s, Ronnie introduced a new component to Sno-Wizard's equipment business—commercial syrups. He bought an existing syrup business and used his fine-tuned palate to significantly expand the company's lineup of flavors. Piña colada was one of the first. "It was one of my favorite drinks, so I started thinking about what went into one, and how you could correlate that with chemical and natural extracts," says Ronnie. "I kept notes on the percentages, and kept tasting the syrup against the real thing."

Under Sciortino's direction, SnoWizard now offers about 140 syrups, including classic New Orleans flavors nectar, orchid cream, and Creole cream cheese, as well as flavors for growing markets in Texas, such as cherimoya, dulce de leche, and tamarind. Ronnie spends months and even years developing a new flavor, making infinitesimal adjustments down to parts-per-million until the concentrate tastes like the item he is mimicking. In the case of cherimoya, a tropical fruit not widely available in New Orleans, he mail-ordered a case and began tasting tiny slivers as he worked in the company's large laboratory. The fruit's diverse combination of flavors emerged on his tongue—banana, peach, strawberry, apple, and bubblegum, among others—and Ronnie scribbled possible formulas for replicating it. He loves this part of the job, an extension of his belief in culinary precision. Even when he's making a forgiving dish like red beans and rice at home, Ronnie uses a scale to measure his dry seasonings down to the gram.

Smartly dressed and sitting near displays of the snoball machines his uncle invented at the SnoWizard headquarters, Ronnie tells me that a lot of people get into the snoball business thinking it's going to be easy money, but they learn fast that strong sales depend on good snoballs. And good snoballs depend on three factors.

Number one, he says, is the temperature of the ice, which has to be kept at five to ten degrees above freezing. If it's too hard when it hits the blades, the shaved ice comes out like talcum powder. If the ice is too soft, the shavings will clump.

The second factor is the sharpness of blades. A good operator sharpens his blades religiously because when the blades dull they produce hard chunks, not soft flurries.

And the third factor is the operator himself, who holds sway over the quality of the confection simply by the way he runs the machine. When the blades are sharp and the ice is right, light pressure is best. But these conditions change every minute of the day, requiring the operator to work by feel.

At Williams Plum Street Snoballs on the corner of Burdette and Plum streets in uptown New Orleans, a line sprawls down the block throughout the spring and summer. New Orleanians have gravitated here since 1945 for snoballs served in a classic oyster pail, the paper carton better known today as a Chinese take-out container.

The oyster-pail tradition was introduced by the stand's founder, Sydney Williams. Claude and Donna Black bought the business in 1979 and have made snoballs to order ever since, forming relationships with steady regulars who have pledged their loyalty to this particular stand. "I don't always remember someone's name, but I remember what flavor they like," Donna admits.

Strawberry is the perennial favorite at Plum Street, as it is at many stands across the city and state. The Blacks still make several flavors created by Williams himself. One is chocolate, composed not from commercial chocolate syrup but made on site from a cocoa powder base. They also make the classic New Orleans flavor orchid cream. Dyed pale purple, it tastes like French vanilla ice cream. Over the years, the Blacks have added several other flavors, including coffee, ice cream, bananas Foster, and king cake, all produced with homemade extracts they make in a kitchen area behind the shop's main counter. They also make condensed milk from scratch. "We're like mad scientists back there," Donna tells me one weekday afternoon, right after she's sized me up to like mango snoballs.

The Chinese take-out container is Plum Street's defining feature and the vessel preferred by the stand's traditionalists. A plastic bag lines the pail to prevent spillage. Claude says it demands the simultaneous use of the spoon and straw. "You have to sip it to keep up with the juice so it won't overflow," he says. I start in on my mango snoball to test his theory.

The Blacks usually open Plum Street the day after Mardi Gras, Ash Wednesday. Once the floats, beads, and king cakes recede, it's time for another seasonal pastime. As the weeks pass and the spring progresses, the line at Plum Street grows longer. Crowds are steady throughout the summer. Knowing when to close the stand in the early fall takes a certain amount of discernment, honed by years of reading their customers' collective mood and paying attention to the weather. By the end of the season, life patterns have changed. Children have returned to school; college students at nearby Tulane and Loyola universities are back in class; and the heat promises to fade. The Blacks never really know in advance when they're going to close for the season. One day, it just makes sense.

⸺⸗⸻

Back at Hansen's, Ashley prepares for the afternoon onslaught of customers. She has been working at the snoball stand since she was a teenager and knows what to do to get ready for the crowd. The syrups have to be mixed, the blocks of ice staged in the chest freezers, the empty paper cups (they don't use Styrofoam) organized by size.

With Ashley's help, Ernest and Mary Hansen were able to stay involved in the business of the stand until their respective deaths shortly after Hurricane Katrina in 2005. The following spring, when it seemed especially important to resume the city's regular rhythms, Ashley opened for the first time by herself. New Orleans clamored for the comfort of culinary rituals, for reminders of seasons past before the storm's epic impact. Compared to the well-documented flooding in the low-lying areas of New Orleans, the uptown neighborhood around Hansen's made it through the storm with minimal damage, and the stand itself was unharmed. One by one, longtime customers trickled in for snoballs and learned that Ernest and Mary had died within months of each other. Many left tributes outside the shop. The Hansens had each lived past ninety years of age.

Ashley continued to open the stand in subsequent seasons, sad for the loss of her grandparents but pleased to carry on the tradition. But by 2008, she realized something grim: Ernest's Sno-Bliz machine was struggling. Its normal steady hum was rattled and labored. In the past, Ernest had maintained the machine himself, making minor adjustments to keep it running smoothly. Now Ashley was fearful it needed work, and she didn't know whom to trust to fix it.

Snoball stands in Louisiana use modern, commercial ice-shaving machines, most of which are produced and serviced by New Orleans companies. But Hansen's is different. Ernest built a handful of machines over the years, all with slightly different designs. Two operate on a daily basis at the shop, the countertop workhorse that makes the majority of the snoballs and a portable machine Ashley takes to catering jobs. The workhorse needed attention.

Panicking, Ashley rifled through her desk for a business card belonging to Richard Cahn, a well-known New Orleans businessman and a friend of her grandparents. Ashley knew that Cahn had a friend named Don Elbers, a chemistry professor at Southeastern Louisiana University, fifty-five miles northwest in Hammond, Louisiana, who had a passion for fixing vintage machines. Elbers had completed several high-profile restoration projects, including the New Orleans City Park carousel organ, a 1917 Model T fire engine, and the calliopes on three vintage Mississippi River steamboats, the *Delta Queen*, the *Mississippi Queen*, and the *American Queen*.

When Ashley approached him, Elbers was reluctant to take the job. He had never worked on a snoball machine, and he appreciated the gravity of the assignment. Hansen's Sno-Bliz was an icon. Still, he liked a challenge and Ashley needed help. He ultimately agreed. "The machine was a mess," Elbers told me. "I'm sure Mr. Hansen never imagined it would still be in use this long. Once he was no longer there to do the maintenance, its condition just continued to get worse."

Elbers thought the machine was well-made and had an impressive design; it had simply been taxed by years of continual use. With Ashley's reluctant permission, he took the ice shaver back to his workshop in Hammond during the snoball off-season and studied its nuances, quirks, and rhythms. At times, he would lay awake at night considering Ernest Hansen's original design decisions. Much of the machine was still solid and aligned, and the angles of the blades were impressively positioned. He wanted to ensure that any adjustments and improvements made in one spot wouldn't alter the functionality somewhere else.

Ashley stayed awake at night, too, worrying about its safe return. The machine was, after all, a family relic, a piece of culinary history, and a source of her family's livelihood.

In the spring, Elbers called to say the machine was fully restored from base to top, and Ashley drove to Hammond with a cooler of block ice to test it. Cleaned, polished, and restored, the machine gleamed, and when Elbers turned it on, Ashley found it purred the way it had when she was a child.

But there was a problem: the shaved ice wasn't coming out exactly right. Elbers had been confident the machine was fixed, and he was puzzled by Ashley's reaction. Then she realized it was the ice. Even in a cooler, it had softened slightly during the drive.

She took the machine back to the Tchoupitoulas Street stand, positioned it on the countertop, and found a block of *good ice* to send through its blades. Tender flakes shot out. "Finally," Ashley recalled, "the machine was perfect. It was working like I always remembered it."

Snoballs at Home

I admit, it's hard to replicate the soft, tender flakes you can get in an authentic Louisiana snoball stand at home, but creating your own confection is a fun experiment. Today's countertop bar blenders and smoothie makers can produce respectable ice that can be scooped into a pretty glass—or a Styrofoam cup—and doused with homemade syrups. Sometimes, my kids and I pick up plain ice from our favorite neighborhood snoball stands. As Williams Plum Street owner Donna Black believes, good proprietors are like mad scientists who appreciate the urge to mix and blend flavors. Prepare your snoballs by combining simple syrup, made by bringing equal parts of water and sugar to a boil, along with flavor extracts that you can purchase or make yourself. Pour some sweet condensed milk into your snoball, or add a scoop of vanilla ice cream between layers of ice for full effect.

Nectar Snoballs

Serves 2.

> 4 cups ice, crushed in a blender to as fine a consistency as
>   possible
> 2 cups nectar syrup (recipe follows)

Spoon the crushed ice into two glasses, stopping halfway up each glass. Pour ½ cup nectar syrup over ice in each glass. Fill glasses with remaining ice, and pour rest of syrup on top.

Nectar Syrup

Makes 1 cup.

> 1 cup white sugar
> 1 cup water

2 teaspoons vanilla extract
1 teaspoon almond extract
½ teaspoon red food coloring

Combine the sugar and water in a saucepan and bring to a boil. Stir
until the sugar is completely dissolved. Add the extracts and the red
food coloring. Remove from heat. When cool, place in a clean container
with a tightly fitted lid and refrigerate.

Kumquat Snoballs

Many of us in south Louisiana grow citrus in our backyards, including
grapefruits, oranges, lemons, satsumas, and kumquats. My kitchen
garden holds two kumquat trees, whose fruit begins to ripen in mid-fall.
I can't resist a kumquat's tart-tangy flesh and edible skin. It's great for
one-bite snacking, but it's even better for incorporating into all sorts of
recipes, including kumquat snoballs.

Serves 4–6.

2 cups sugar
2 cups water
About 25–30 kumquats, sliced in half, seeds removed
Crushed ice
12-ounce can condensed milk

Combine sugar and water in a saucepan and bring to a boil. Whisk well,
until sugar is completely dissolved. Add kumquat slices and simmer
for about 20 minutes. Remove from heat and cool completely. Strain
candied kumquats from the simple syrup using a strainer. Reserve fruit.
Pour liquid into a clean container with a tightly fitted lid and refrigerate. Fill 4 glasses with crushed ice. Pour enough simple syrup to soak
the ice well. Add 3 tablespoons of condensed milk into the ice in each
glass. Garnish with candied kumquats.

5

By the Full Moon in August
Filé

Lionel Key sits erect in a metal folding chair in the Louisiana Folklife Village, the area for traditional craftspeople at the New Orleans Jazz and Heritage Festival. His knees are spread, and between them is a 120-pound carved cypress mortar. From a distance, it looks like a good-sized tree stump. Lionel's beefy hands are wrapped around a companion pestle, a four-foot long solid wood instrument rounded on each end. He raises and lowers the pestle into a bed of dried sassafras leaves resting in the mortar's scooped bottom. Within a minute or two, his rhythmic pounding has reduced the crisp leaves to tiny flakes, like crumbs left behind in a potato chip bag. Then he flips the pestle over and, using its smaller end, he grinds the flakes until they are fine and powdery. The green dust that remains is filé, the spice used to season and thicken gumbo for as long as gumbo itself has been made in Louisiana—nearly three hundred years. That's plenty of time for filé to secure a place in the state's culinary repertoire and to inspire its own distinct set of rituals.

Most filé found in and around Louisiana is produced by commercial food manufacturers. A small amount, however, is made by artisan producers like Lionel who make it by hand and who spring from the state's tradition of grinding filé at home to accompany gumbo. Traditionally, rural families foraged for sassafras leaves in the late summer, dried the leaves in a cool, dark place, and later ground them into filé powder. Lionel learned the craft from his great-uncle, a fact he shares with festival goers who drop by his booth. Surrounding him on this humid Saturday afternoon are other examples of Louisiana folk traditions: Mardi Gras float making, African American quilting, and edible St. Joseph altars arranged every March by the descendants of New Orleans's Sicilian immigrants.

While Lionel raises and lowers his pestle, live music pulses through the air from the various stages situated around the Fair Grounds Race Course, the one-mile thoroughbred racetrack in the Mid-City neighborhood of New Orleans where Jazz Fest takes place every spring. Savory aromas waft through the breeze from nearly sixty food booths. Hamburgers, hot dogs, funnel cakes, and other colorless festival eats were outlawed long ago; Jazz Fest food vendors sell only Cajun, Creole, or international cuisines traceable to the Louisiana melting pot. As the crowd moves lazily around him, Lionel drives the pestle deep into the mortar, exchanging pleasantries with strangers and acquaintances. By the time he packs up his equipment and heads home to Baton Rouge at the end of the weekend, Lionel will have explained his longtime craft to hundreds of visitors and sold every one of his hexagonal glass jars of handmade filé. "I can tell right away if somebody is from Louisiana or not," he tells me. "They look at my filé and the first thing they say is, 'Is it spicy?'" He pauses, and a look of mild amusement crawls across his tawny face. "I say, 'No. It ain't spicy.'"

He tells a couple from the Midwest that filé has a flavor that's hard to pin down, that it's just one of those things you have to try in gumbo, and that once you do, you can't live without it. He opens a small glass jar and lets the wife sniff the fine powder inside. Its aroma is grassy with subtle citrus notes. They buy a jar and move on, joking about how now they'll have to learn to make gumbo. Lionel resumes pounding, and I can feel his dull thumps through the earth below.

Like an Old World alchemist, he grabs more leaves from a burlap sack, adds them to the mortar's pit, and continues to grind. Even native Louisianans milling about the festival are intrigued to see his unusual equipment. They are well aware of filé, and some have even prepared it themselves, but a mortar and pestle like Lionel's are rare. His tools are heirlooms handed down from his great-uncle Joseph Willie "Uncle Bill" Ricard. Born blind, Ricard began making and selling handmade filé near Baton Rouge in 1904 after his uncle fashioned a large mortar and pestle that the youngster could use with ease.

Filé is believed to have been produced by Choctaw Indians, who lived in Louisiana in large numbers. Many Choctaw lived along the west bank of the Mississippi River near Pointe Coupee north of Baton Rouge, as well as the southern portions of the Ouachita, Boeuf, and Tensas rivers in north Louisiana. Smaller groups lived along the Pearl River north of New Orleans. Collectively, the Choctaw grew to be a large tribe widespread across the state. They often conducted business with settlers, selling them wild game and medicinal plants and herbs for home remedies. After the New Orleans French Market was established in 1813, some traveled by dugout canoe to trade with settlers there, displaying filé on blankets at the market.

The ground spice was sourced from *Sassafras albidum,* a deciduous North American tree belonging to the laurel family that is still common in the eastern and southern United States. Its hand-shaped leaves released natural aromas that prompted the Choctaw and other Native American tribes, eager for culinary variation, to incorporate it into their diets to enhance flavor. By then, indigenous peoples in the United States were using sassafras for medicinal purposes as well.

The sassafras tree is, of course, also associated with root beer. Its roots and bark impart a starkly different flavor from its leaves, and these were used in root beer production as far back as colonial America. Extracts from sassafras roots and bark were used in root beer until 1960 when the U.S. Food and Drug Administration labeled them carcinogens and banned their use. Before the cancer scare, some Cajun families dug wild sassafras roots to make tea. Despite the warning, some still do.

By the time the Choctaw were selling their filé at the New Orleans French Market, gumbo—and filé itself—had become entrenched in the city's culinary scene. Gumbo's origins are still debated, but it is likely a combination of African, French, and Native American cooking traditions. Most food historians place gumbo's establishment in Louisiana in the early 1720s. By then, slaves had arrived from West Africa and large groups of French colonists were establishing residences in New Orleans, then the colony's capital. French colonists and slaves interacted over available ingredients and cooking methods, and they tapped indigenous tribes for information on what to eat, grow, and collect. Culinary traditions naturally began to fuse and adapt. The slaves, who were probably gumbo's chief architects, arrived with a tradition of stews and a fondness for okra, a plant plentiful in West Africa that was transplanted to Louisiana's tropical climate. They also introduced the practice of eating stews with rice. French colonists brought an awareness of bouillabaisse, an on-the-spot fish soup pioneered by Provençal fishermen that incorporated extra or inferior ingredients from the daily catch. And Native Americans brought knowledge of local seafood, game, and wild foliage, including sassafras leaves.

Filé, with its gentle lemony notes, was indeed aromatic, but it offered something practical to the colonists and slaves as well: the power to thicken. Added to gumbo, filé imparted a feeling of satiety. Today, if a native Louisianan, or anyone acquainted with the spice, is asked to describe its purpose, *to flavor and to thicken* tumbles forth like a childhood recitation. The widely held belief that filé thickens gumbo is no joke. Like okra, sassafras leaves contain a high level of mucilage, a gluey substance found to varying degrees in different plants. Complex sugar molecules within the mucilage called polysaccharides are responsible for the thickening. They attract and combine with water molecules in the gumbo's broth, making the liquid more viscous. A few generous pinches of filé, followed by stirring, leads to a perceptible change in gumbo's consistency.

Some high-profile chefs, including Emeril Lagasse, have mentioned filé on national cooking shows and in their own cookbooks. And culinary blogs and on-line discussions about regional foodstuffs have made it easy for anyone to learn about filé, including how to identify *S. albidum* and dry and grind leaves at home. Still, filé is a spice largely confined to Louisiana and its gumbo culture. And within this small world, Lionel is one of a few remaining boutique producers.

⌒⌒

Over lunch at Parrain's Restaurant in Baton Rouge, Lionel and I catch up on how the filé business has been lately. We got to know each other several years ago, when I began covering Louisiana's artisan food producers. Of Creole descent, Lionel grew up in Baton Rouge watching his Uncle Bill use the famed mortar and pestle at Bill's home at the western edge of the city's Garden District, the neighborhood where I live today. Bill's house is no longer there; the lot is occupied by spindly trees. He had been born in the rural community of Rougon (pronounced Roo-gon), twenty-five miles northwest of town, and had moved to Baton Rouge as an adult. Filé, along with a broom- and mop-making venture, helped him provide for his wife, nicknamed "Sweet," and their four children.

It wasn't until Lionel was in his thirties and working as a UPS driver that he asked his uncle for a turn at the mortar and pestle. Bill agreed, and Lionel took a seat and began to pound. To Bill, the strokes sounded flinty and insubstantial. "He'd say, 'My boo. You're not hitting it right,'" Lionel told me. "'You got to hit it in the *center*.'" When the pestle finally made proper contact, Bill gave his approval.

A few years after Lionel's first lesson, Bill died and left his nephew the prized equipment. Eventually, Lionel quit his job and began making and selling filé himself, labeling his product Uncle Bill's Creole Filé. Since then, he has sold hundreds of jars a year at farmers markets and festivals around the state.

Filé production hasn't been a big money maker, and as Lionel gets older, the physical demands of the craft are becoming more challenging. A man of modest means who now lives in an apartment in a depressed Baton Rouge neighborhood, he relies on laborious seasonal foraging for his raw materials.

Year after year, the process is the same, he tells me over lunch—seafood gumbo and shrimp fettuccine for him, and a shrimp po'boy for me. He goes without filé today because he has forgotten to bring one of his jars along, and he won't use the commercial kind at the restaurant. Lionel is not a landowner, so he trudges to locations along state highways and rural roads where sassafras trees grow. Sometimes he visits plots owned by his cousins outside Baton Rouge, but more often, he heads for wild roadside groves scouted by friends and acquaintances—land whose owners Lionel never meets. He won't divulge exactly where or when he harvests sassafras leaves, but the lore surrounding filé suggests it occurs near the full moon in August, although filé maker Stacy Bonnecaze, who sells the spice at farmers markets in Baton Rouge and New Orleans along with hand-ground cornmeal and red pepper, says she harvests the leaves in September. In any case, the harvest is coordinated with filé's principal dish. By the time the sassafras leaves are plucked, dried, and finely ground, it is about time for fall and winter gumbo.

Lionel tells me that he looks for a tree whose branches are reachable, and he lops off as many thin ones as he can carry and walks them back to the flatbed of his pickup truck. When the bed is full, he heads home, hanging the branches to dry for an undisclosed amount of time. Ideally, he gathers two or three truckloads at the outset of the season to give him enough to last. I've asked him many times how long he allows the leaves to cure, but the answer is always the same. "I can't tell you all my secrets," he says again today, peering at me over lowered spectacles.

When he is ready to make filé, Lionel plucks the dried leaves from the branches and drops them into the mortar, filling it halfway. The ends of the pestle are made from two different woods, ash and pecan, fused together at the center. Once he has finished pounding and grinding,

Lionel removes the ground filé and sifts it through two different mesh screens to remove textural inconsistencies. Then he spoons it into glass jars of three different sizes and boxes them up for markets, festivals, or face-to-face sales.

When he's not selling filé, Lionel works as a driver for friends and acquaintances who don't have transportation. His red pickup truck wears a magnetic sign advertising filé, inviting occasional phone calls from motorists. "I've had several people call me on the road, so I always keep some with me," he says.

⌒ℤ⌒

To fully understand the tradition of filé requires a close look at gumbo, the one and only dish with which it is associated. Like fried chicken or chili elsewhere, gumbo is a dish made by generations of families in Louisiana. Highly variable and intensely personal, the preparation of gumbo is hotly debated, and the debate itself is part of this dish's enduring charm.

Over the course of its history, gumbo has depended on at-hand ingredients, some lowly and some fancy, which come together under the cook's confident direction. Whatever its final composition, gumbo begins with a roux, the thick base made by cooking and stirring equal parts of flour and oil until it reaches a preferred shade of brown. The enduring purpose of roux is simple: It ensures gumbo has a consistency thicker and more viscous than an ordinary stock-based soup. It also gives gumbo its characteristic muddy hue.

Once the roux is finished, there are broad variations about what, and when, to add next. Many cooks sauté the Holy Trinity—chopped onions, green bell peppers, and celery—with the roux. Others sauté them separately. Whatever the method, these aromatic vegetables make their way into the gumbo pot, along with water or broth and the proteins that give the gumbo its identity.

Classic gumbo combinations include chicken or duck paired with smoked pork sausage or andouille; shrimp and okra; or seafood, which can mean crawfish, crabmeat, whole "gumbo" crabs, crab fingers, oysters, shrimp, and hunks of filleted fish. Gumbo made from a Thanksgiving turkey carcass is a requisite part of the holiday in many Louisiana households.

Gumbo is most often made by gut and feel, but some notable recipes in Louisiana are more formulaic. Donaldsonville-based chef and restaurateur John Folse famously created a dish, called Death by Gumbo, for then–*New York Times* columnist and Mississippi native Craig Claiborne that featured gumbo broth poured over deboned bobwhite quail. This creation, served with rice cooked with filé, has been featured on the menu of his newest restaurant, R'evolution, in the French Quarter. And beloved New Orleans restaurateur Leah Chase of Dooky Chase, whose life story inspired the Disney movie *The Princess and the Frog,* is known for her green gumbo or Gumbo Z'Herbes, a Holy Thursday Catholic tradition in Louisiana, particularly in New Orleans. It is made from a painfully long list of leafy green vegetables and meats including chicken, sausage, beef, and pork, and it is served as a bit of indulgence before the Catholic Good Friday fast.

Generally, though, there is broad variation among chefs, in households, and in cookbooks about what finally lands in the pot. Some gumbo cooks like to incorporate okra. Others prefer to leave it out. Creole gumbos that spring from New Orleans often feature both okra and tomatoes, but the Cajun gumbos from the parishes west of Lafayette usually do not. Some cooks take great pains to make their own stock. Others declare the secret is to toss in tiny chunks of inexpensive lunchmeat, a habit that derives from the long-standing use of ham in gumbo in the first half of the twentieth century.

Gumbo isn't gumbo without cooked white rice and—no surprise— there is also debate about the best way to serve this part of the dish. For some, rice is best served by spooning it into the bowl first, with the steaming liquid poured on top. Other cooks serve an ice cream scoop of rice atop the gumbo or in a tiny dish on the side, so it can be added a little at a time.

Indeed, gumbo is a food that invites frivolous rituals: the arrangement of rice, the application of hot sauce and extra salt and pepper, the dipping of French bread. In some regions of the state, satellite dishes of creamy potato salad or a baked sweet potato are served with gumbo, so that spoonsful can be plopped into the bowl to add flavor and alter consistency—but, most of all, to stretch the ceremony further.

Similarly, the use of filé is ritualized and debated. Since filé and okra are both natural thickeners, most gumbo cooks think it overkill to use both. Others believe a good roux is the only element required to achieve proper viscosity and use neither. As for when to add filé, many swear by the principle that it must be added at the table only, because cooking with it can make gumbo "stringy" or gummy. Others, including Lionel, shun the warning and believe a teaspoon or two should be added to the pot during the simmering process.

By nature, gumbo is a robust dish thanks to the sturdiness of roux, the assertiveness of the onion, celery, and bell pepper, and the redoubtable presence of more than one protein. Filé adds a distinct finish—an earthy, herbal counterpoint to this burly mix. Thin jars of filé powder are staples on the tables of south Louisiana restaurants that take their gumbo seriously.

※

I'm gathering research and driving south on Highway 24 from the bayou town of Schriever one February afternoon when I spot a white plywood sign with stenciled black letters that reads "Fresh Gumbo Filé for Sale." This is one of the things I love about Louisiana, its supply of culinary cottage industries. I've lost count of the hand-painted signs I've seen over the years, advertising everything from fresh shrimp and strawberries to fresh 'coon and gasper goo (fresh-water drum). The filé sign is staked at the edge of the property of Earl Gaudet, a hardscrabble retired laborer who once worked fabricating fiberglass living quarters for offshore oilrigs in the Gulf.

Earl lives in a mobile home on four acres of land—a large plot by suburban standards, but nothing unusual here. It is all that remains from an original 1,800-acre swath his Cajun descendants once owned and farmed. Across the highway from his tidy homestead are St. Bridget's Catholic Church, Schriever Elementary School (which he once attended), and a seafood market whose movable-type sign advertises 'fat females.' It's a reference to blue crabs netted in nearby estuaries.

Earl tells me that he sells his filé in a few local grocery stores and restaurants and in the gift shop of Laura Plantation, an 1805 sugar plantation in adjacent St. James Parish. Most of his customers, however, are people who spot his sign while motoring along the state road. When the weather cools, the mood for gumbo intensifies and passersby turn down his dirt driveway.

An avid hunter, gardener, and fisherman, Earl is a study in self-sufficiency. His pantry and freezer are stocked almost solely by his own efforts. An expansive shed nearly as big as his mobile home protects the fishing boat he takes out regularly to Pointe-aux-Chenes, an area in the coastal wetlands south of Houma. The shed also covers pens of his dozen or so beagles and Treeing Walker Coonhounds, boisterous hunting companions that join him on expeditions for deer and rabbit in the woods nearby. His flat, open yard allows for a sunbathed year-round garden in which different seasonal vegetables grow. Just beyond the garden is his personal grove of about thirty sassafras trees, most of which he uprooted from the area's swampy lowlands and moved to his land. "That's the only way you can get a sassafras tree, is from a swamp," Earl says, sucking deeply on a cigarette. "But I tell you, that is one tree that is hard to transplant. One time I planted eighteen trees, but only five took."

The dogs bark in mad succession as Earl and I pass their pens and head toward his sassafras grove. The tallest trees are about eight feet.

Right now the trees are denuded, but in the spring their lobed leaves will burst out. As the heat intensifies throughout the summer, the leaves will grow larger and turn from pale to dark green.

Earl's method of filé production, handed down from his mother, involves picking the leaves from the trees and spreading them in a single layer on one of several six-foot tables under the shelter of the shed. Once he has arranged them, he covers the leaves with netting to keep them from blowing away. This is flat, open territory, and the wind can whip up unexpectedly. The leaves remain there drying for three to four days, until they become what he calls "crispy crispy."

Then Earl places the leaves into a pillowcase made of blue-and-white mattress ticking, a fabric he says is durable enough to handle his next step. He beats the bag with a baseball bat against the side of the concrete steps that lead to his trailer's side door, manipulating the pillowcase further with his hands to ensure the leaves are finely ground. Afterward, he sifts the filé through a fine screen. The finished product is powdery but has the tiny textural variations that come from hand production. I open one of the small jars I'm buying from him and smell its sweet aroma, which reminds me of tea leaves and faintly, lemon peel. Earl will make filé several times throughout the fall, filling as many as one thousand four-ounce jars that he sells for $5 each. "You pay more when you get it like this, but it's good stuff," he says. "A lot of people use my filé. It goes from California to the East Coast."

Earl opens a small photo album on the tiny, square kitchen table in his trailer. The album documents each of his production steps, and he keeps it ready to show customers. Most of them are well acquainted with filé, but they like seeing someone produce it by hand.

About that time, we hear the crunch of car tires against the gravel and ground oyster shells that line Earl's driveway. A gleaming white Cadillac creeps to a halt, and a well-dressed woman knocks on the door. I hear her ask Earl if he still has filé. She smiles when he says yes.

"Good," she says. "'Cause I need twenty-four jars."

Seafood Gumbo

My husband John's longtime favorite version of gumbo is seafood, and we've spent years perfecting a version brimming with Louisiana's bounty. The trick to successful seafood gumbo is to take the time to establish a rich, flavorful broth on the front end. To achieve this, I use fresh, head-on large shrimp and make stock with the heads and shells, adding it to my roux, along with sautéed vegetables. Once this liquid base is complete, the final step is adding delicate fresh seafood. I turn off the heat immediately so that the tender shrimp, oysters, and crabmeat won't overcook. Because my version of seafood gumbo contains no okra, its lineage is primarily Cajun, but I've included a cup of fresh chopped tomatoes for sweetness, which springs from Creole gumbos. It's a happy marriage.

Serves 8–10.

    2 pounds large head-on shrimp
    2 yellow onions, peeled and quartered
    3 stalks celery with leaves, cut into 2-inch pieces
    3 whole carrots, peeled and cut into 2-inch pieces
    1 tablespoon peppercorns
    1 ½ tablespoons kosher salt
    4 bay leaves
    ½ cup roux (see page 000)
    1 medium yellow onion, chopped
    1 red, yellow, or orange bell pepper, chopped
    1 green bell pepper, chopped
    3 stalks celery, trimmed and chopped, leaves included
    3 cloves garlic, minced
    10 cups shellfish stock (prepared from shrimp shells)
    6 bay leaves
    16 ounces crab fingers

16 ounces crabmeat (claw, backfin, or lump)
32 ounces shucked oysters
1 cup chopped fresh tomatoes
Salt and ground black pepper to taste
Cooked rice and fresh or jarred filé for serving

Peel and devein shrimp, reserving heads and shells. Place reserved heads and shells into a stockpot and add next three ingredients. Fill with 12 cups water and bring to a boil. Add peppercorns, salt, and bay leaves. Simmer for 45–60 minutes.

While stock is simmering, prepare roux. Once completed, add chopped onion, bell peppers, celery, and minced garlic and sauté until soft. Slowly add homemade shrimp stock, whisking to incorporate roux. Add bay leaves, and simmer for 30 minutes. Taste for seasoning.

While gumbo broth simmers, clean and prepare remaining seafood by removing loose shells from crab fingers, crab meat, and oysters. Add seafood and tomatoes to pot and remove from heat. They will poach without overcooking. After about 10 minutes, taste and adjust seasonings. Serve with rice and fresh filé.

Turkey Bone Gumbo

I grew up in Georgia, and the memorable soups of my childhood were not gumbo, but two different forms of vegetable soup. My maternal grandmother made a brothy vegetable beef soup fragrant with bay and chock-full of diminutive peas, corn, and lima beans that would convene at the bottom of my bowl. I loved gobbling them up last. And my paternal grandfather was famous for ham vegetable soup that featured fresh smoked ham, lots of cabbage, tomatoes, and turnips. My first enduring impression of gumbo came years later, when I was a college student in Washington, D.C. A friend of mine there was a native Louisianan who had recently parted ways with his girlfriend, also a Bayou State native. He was heartbroken, but not about the relationship. My friend had left behind turkey bone gumbo the two had made in their Capitol Hill apartment after Thanksgiving. It had reminded them of the flavors of home and had turned out so well that it rivaled their mothers' versions. Neither was willing to give up the remaining frozen stash. With authentic, homemade gumbo a rare find outside of Louisiana, a custody dispute was underway that was the talk among other Louisianans working on the Hill that year. I was intrigued by the chokehold this humble dish seemed to have on its fans.

I've been making my own gumbos for years, inspired by my Louisiana in-laws. Turkey bone gumbo is a standard around our house after Thanksgiving.

½ cup roux (see page 000)
1 yellow onion, diced
1 red bell pepper, diced
1 green bell pepper, diced
3 stalks celery with leaves, chopped
3 garlic cloves, peeled and minced
12-ounce andouille, sliced into half-inch pieces
10 cups turkey stock (recipe follows)

6 bay leaves

4 cups turkey meat, reserved from carcass

6 green onions, green parts chopped

Fresh parsley to taste

Cooked rice and fresh or jarred filé for serving

In a large pot, make roux. Add diced vegetables and sauté until soft, about 5 minutes. Add andouille and sauté for another 5 minutes. Slowly add turkey stock, whisking to thoroughly incorporate roux. Add bay leaves. Bring to a boil. Reduce heat and simmer 20 minutes. Add turkey and let cook for another 10 minutes. Serve with rice, chopped green onions, parsley, and fresh or jarred filé.

Turkey Stock

1 roast turkey carcass, leftover meat removed and reserved. Leave a little meat on the bone to add flavor to the stock.

3 large yellow or white onions, peeled and quartered

4 stalks celery, including leaves, cut into two-inch pieces

4 large carrots, peeled and cut into two-inch pieces

1 tablespoon black peppercorns

6 bay leaves

3–5 tablespoons salt, or to taste

Several sprigs of fresh thyme and Italian parsley, tied in a bundle with kitchen twine

Place carcass in a large stockpot and cover with cold water. Add onions, celery, carrots, black peppercorns, and bay leaves and bring to boil. Lower heat to simmer and add salt and herb bundle. Simmer 40 minutes. Turn off heat. Taste and adjust seasoning level if necessary. Drain stock through a mesh strainer and skim fat from surface. The stock can be used now, or it can be refrigerated for one week or frozen for three months.

6

Blood Sausage at Sunrise
Red Boudin

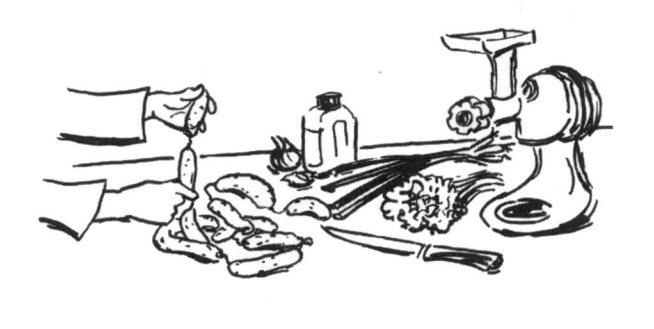

On a stainless steel prep table in the back of a weathered meat market seventy miles south of Baton Rouge sits an open sleeve of saltine crackers and, on a piece of butcher paper, a single link of blood boudin. The link was left there for me by a fourth-generation Cajun butcher named Beau Bourgeois, who, along with his father Donald and several of the meat market's employees, spent the early morning hours making hundreds of pounds of boudin here in the bayou town of Schriever.

Beau is a focused young man who passed on a Ph.D. program in mathematics at Tulane University to move home and join his dad in the family business, Bourgeois's Meat Market. Founded in 1891, Bourgeois's sits on the bustling state highway that serves as Schriever's main street, and it is identified by a faded wooden sign that includes the tagline "Miracles in Meat." Generations of locals have shopped here for Bourgeois's boudin, Cajun meats, and homemade beef jerky. The smoked items are prepared in a rickety manual smokehouse out back that has no fancy dials—only small moveable fireboxes filled with smoldering hardwood that Donald replenishes every two hours. In the case of the jerky, he slides the boxes around on the smokehouse floor to make sure the heat reaches hundreds of beef strips draped on tiny nails above. Bourgeois's jerky is wildly popular among the area's numerous offshore oil industry salesmen. They tell Donald the stuff is like catnip for grumpy secretaries. Bourgeois's is also one of the last remaining places in Louisiana to produce blood boudin.

Sometimes referred to as *boudin noir* or red boudin (despite the faulty translation of colors), Louisiana's blood boudin is a diminishing subset of the otherwise vigorous boudin culture. Today, dozens of roadside Cajun butchers and small grocery stores produce boudin, a fresh Cajun sausage composed of braised, ground pork, usually pig's liver, white rice, pork broth, spices, and aromatic vegetables combined and stuffed in a casing. On the rare occasions it's sold alongside blood boudin, it's called white boudin or *boudin blanc*. Most of the time, it's just called boudin.

Louisiana's red and white boudins spring from Old World sausage-making techniques imported by French, Acadian, and German immigrants. The pig became a fundamental part of the diets of these farmers, who followed tried-and-true methods of using every bit of the animal—blood included—in their local charcuterie. Boudin was just one resulting product. Early butchers made a version of the French smoked sausage *andouille* and seasoned smoked shoulder meat they called *tasso*. These frugal farmers fried pork skin in rendered fat to make cracklins, and they produced hog's head cheese, a gelatinous terrine-like dish made from meat from the pig's head and bone marrow that springs from country pâté. They also stuffed the stomach of a pig with ground pork, rice, and spices to produce a dish called *chaudin*, *ponce*, or *gog* depending on the part of the state where it was produced. The word "gog" probably derives from the Anjou blood sausage *gogues*, even though the Cajun version contained no blood.

I pick up the plump, garnet-hued link and pierce one end with my front teeth, enough to open a hole in the translucent casing. With the help of the same gentle thumb pressure you would apply to a tube of Crest, I ease the pork, rice, and cooked blood filling onto an awaiting cracker. Most boudin consumers don't eat the casing; the yummy stuff inside must be squeezed out. Boudin lovers are happy to demonstrate to the uninitiated exactly how the process works, and if you've learned to love this road food as an adult, as I have, you cleave to your first boudin moment. Mine occurred a year after I moved to Louisiana, when a naturalist friend and fellow LSU graduate student took me birding in the rice fields around Rayne to watch the migratory water fowl that stop off in Louisiana throughout the winter. On the way there we stopped at the Best Stop, a famed boudin purveyor in the town of Scott, self-proclaimed boudin capital of the world and home to the state's annual boudin festival. There in the parking lot, like countless others before me, I learned to drag my incisors carefully across the surface of the casing, coaxing the innards out and onto my tongue. Once we finished, my friend and I cast our casings into the nearest garbage can and drove off with a savory haze lingering in our mouths.

Boudin's roadside appeal and quirky consumption procedure are one of Louisiana's most celebrated culinary phenomena, relished by locals and marveled at by visitors. And adding to its mystique, boudin is neither widely available in restaurants nor typically made at home, unlike gumbo, jambalaya, étouffée, and other well-known Louisiana dishes. Producing it is a laborious and protracted process that, thankfully, a healthy number of purveyors are still willing to perform. It's fair to say that more than fifty roadside butchers and convenience stores produce it today across south Louisiana. Order a link and the attendant will pluck it out of a countertop rice steamer or slow cooker with a pair of tongs, swaddle it in butcher paper, and hand it over. It's best consumed within minutes of purchase, either in an idling car in the parking lot or while driving down the road. A greasy sheen on the fingertips is part of the experience; so is a cold beer or root beer to wash it down.

It occurs to me fleetingly as I smear my cracker with Bourgeois's blood boudin that it seems sinful to tear the treat from its casing so soon after it was put there in the first place. Beau, Donald, and three longtime Bourgeois employees had worked for hours early that morning preparing both red and white boudin, a process that started the night before when Donald began simmering 2,500 pounds of bone-in pork shoulder and 60 pounds of pork liver in a steel drum that was positioned over a gas burner in the meat market's prep room.

By sunup the next morning, the pork was cooked and beginning to cool. Donald strained it in small batches and dumped each scoop onto a stainless steel work table, and the workers, dressed in rubber boots and Neoprene aprons, painstakingly separated the steaming meat from the bones, searching for small fragments. Then they sent pound after pound of deboned pork through a large grinder, combining it afterwards with cooked long-grain white rice (you're more likely to get medium-grain rice in the western part of Acadiana), pork broth, salt, black and cayenne pepper, garlic powder, and handfuls of chopped green onions and parsley. About one-sixth of the mixture was set aside for blood boudin. To that, they added a gallon of pig's blood, poured from a plastic milk jug.

The mixtures of boudin—first *blanc* and then *noir*—were loaded into a hydraulic sausage stuffer. One of the store's veterans, Schriever native Calvin Hue, was in charge of this part of the operation. Rookies aren't trusted with the job since it takes a light hand to avoid overfilling—and exploding—a boudin casing. I watched Calvin extract a cleaned pork intestine from a bucket of water where a tangle of them was soaking. Some boudin purveyors have switched to synthetic casings, but Bourgeois's has not. Calvin threaded a twenty-foot-long casing around the mouth of the stuffer, bunching it up like a fat caterpillar until its sealed end was visible. Then he hit a foot pump on the stuffer, triggering the filling to shoot out. The casing came to life like a wind sock in the breeze. Once

Calvin had filled it completely—but not too tightly—he tied off the end and tossed the sausage down the prep table to Donald, Beau, and long-time employee Chris Derocher, who twisted the long length into about six one-pound links whose ends came together in a single knot.

A confident rhythm took over as the men worked, their hands on autopilot while they chatted about LSU football and national politics. They hung each bundle of links onto a tiered hook on a floor-to-ceiling steel rod. The boudin blanc links were ready to sell. The links of boudin noir were steamed in a large kettle until the blood was thoroughly cooked. So much work had gone into constructing the link in front of me, and here I was squirting its contents right back out.

The link of blood boudin was sublime, luscious and disarming. There was nothing "bloody" about it. It was rich and aromatic, and it stood out from boudin blanc the way a burger made with ground tenderloin trumps one made with ground chuck: more complex and deeper in flavor. I found it hard to believe that the legions of boudin enthusiasts both in and outside of Louisiana hadn't jumped on the blood boudin bandwagon. "It's mostly old timers asking for it," Donald told me later. "The young people . . . not too many of them want it."

Bourgeois's got its start as a slaughterhouse and mobile meat market in 1891, when Donald's grandfather Valerie Jean-Batiste Bourgeois decided to become a traveling butcher. Working outside his home on the town's main street, he would slaughter a single pig or cow at a time and load the cuts onto a horse-drawn cart, meeting customers in the small bayou towns in Schriever's orbit. He returned home only when empty-handed.

Eventually, Bourgeois established a commercial slaughterhouse and an accompanying storefront across the street, which is where the meat market still operates. When Bourgeois died in 1949, his son Lester took over the shop, continuing the tradition of sausage making and custom slaughtering for the large numbers of families in the area that kept livestock or hunted. Lester retired in the 1990s, and Donald, who had been working at the meat market since childhood, took over. Lester still lives across the street from the business and checks on operations regularly.

Bourgeois's, like other slaughterhouse-cum-meat markets in southern Louisiana, historically made boudin to use up pork trimmings. Adding blood from the slaughtered animal incorporated another on-hand ingredient and provided an additional dimension of flavor.

While Louisiana's boudin isn't widely available outside of the southern part of the state, it is fairly well known. Calvin Trillin's 2002 column in *The New Yorker*, "Missing Links," shared the writer's longtime devotion to the food and revealed the fervent opinions south Louisianans have about which purveyor's boudin is best. The Southern Foodways Alliance (SFA) and its sweeping Southern Boudin Trail oral history project, which created an online map of boudin sources and documented the perspectives of modern boudin craftspeople, have also bolstered awareness of the dish.

One of the first serious bloggers about boudin is Professor Bob Carriker, a Washington native who fell in love with it while interviewing for a position in the University of Louisiana at Lafayette's Department of History in 1997. A faculty member who escorted him around Lafayette, the largest city in Cajun Country, introduced Bob to boudin.

En route to the airport for his flight back home, Bob's guide took him to a convenience store for a link of boudin. Like any good local, she showed him how to consume the Cajun specialty in the car before they pulled away. Bob followed her example. He found the experience both bizarre and irresistible. "I called my wife right away," he told me recently from his university office. "And I said, 'You are not going to believe what I just did.'"

Bob was offered and accepted the position, and for the next several years from his new home in Lafayette, he visited dozens of roadside meat markets in Cajun Country to taste as many different links as he could. By 2004, he had developed a site called boudinlink.com, where he records comments and assigns letter grades to each sample of boudin. By 2014, he had reviewed more than 170 links of boudin, completed a companion guidebook, and was regularly called upon by regional and national media to comment on the captivating local tradition.

Bob's goal was purely recreational, but his project unwittingly revealed the sheer volume of boudin available in Louisiana. "I'm pretty sure I've sampled more links of boudin than anybody else in the world," says Bob, who chuckles about the amount of feedback his boudin project has received compared to that of his 2010 scholarly work, a book called *Urban Farming in the West: A New Deal Experiment in Subsistence Homesteads.*

His project demonstrates another point. Despite its short and uncomplicated ingredient list, no two versions of boudin taste the same. They vary on several fronts, including the pork-to-rice ratio, the moistness of the link and its residual grease, the level of red and black pepper, how much liver is detected, and to what degree flecks of parsley and chopped scallion show through the translucent casing, enhancing flavor and aesthetics.

Bob's willingness to explore the range of boudin available makes him different from most local boudin consumers, who, like salmon spawning upstream, return to the same roadside shop for generations. "Asking a bunch of Cajuns who's got the best boudin around is the world's easiest conversation starter," he says. "It doesn't matter if they've tried others or not."

Boudin thrives in the two dozen parishes that comprise Cajun Country but is less common in the rest of Louisiana. This regionality only adds to its appeal, prompting statewide fans to road trip to their nearest boudin purveyor to supply football tailgates or to express-mail a care package to homesick family members. Boudin is made further alluring by the fact that it's rarely shipped by retailers because most of them don't want the hassle of USDA regulations. They would rather focus on over-the-counter sales.

Only a few of the boudin purveyors Bob has reviewed over the years have closed, while a surprising number of new ones have opened. Reasonably priced and popular, boudin is Louisiana's first fast food and the anchor product in Cajun meat markets. In the last few decades, some purveyors also began making versions of boudin with crawfish, shrimp and crab, and alligator. Many supply boudin balls as well, spheres of boudin filling that are rolled, breaded, and deep fried until the crust is brown and crisp.

But while Louisiana's boudin culture continues to thrive, blood boudin has not. Between Bob, the SFA, and my own sleuthing, I found only three remaining commercial purveyors in the entire state when I started this project. Blood boudin seems to have met its near-demise for two reasons.

The first is the psychology of taste. As much as they love boudin, younger Louisianans show little interest in a version made with blood. "I don't eat the red," a serious young blonde woman in line at Bourgeois's told me. "No thank you." She wasn't alone. I mentioned my blood boudin research to dozens of boudin enthusiasts, most of them native Louisianans, who almost universally declared that the thought of eating blood sausage made them shudder. "I think the 'yuck factor' definitely has had something to do with it," says Jim Jenkins of the Louisiana Department of Agriculture and Forestry, who has worked closely with the state's small butchers and slaughterhouses for decades.

Ironically, trendy recipes that incorporate blood may be on the rise elsewhere. In 2011, the celebrated Toronto restaurant Buca earned high international praise for its *torta di sanguinaccio,* a southern Italian pastry in which the custard is made with chocolate and tempered blood. That same year, a summer issue of *Food Arts* magazine featured a cover story that explored the history and modern culinary application of blood. And in Louisiana—as blood boudin waned in Cajun Country—a stylish new festival celebrating boudin sprouted in New Orleans that included samples of the Italian blood sausage *biroldo,* prepared by one of the festival's organizers, Chef Mario Batali.

But even if modern consumers suddenly became inspired to embrace blood boudin, another factor has repressed it in Louisiana. In the 1970s, local meat markets, many of which were also slaughterhouses, faced arduous new state and federal regulations for meat inspection. Among other things, the regulations required the blood used in blood boudin to come from an animal slaughtered in front of an inspector. Many Cajun meat markets, especially those that were getting out of the slaughter business anyway, consequently shut down their blood boudin production. Some dual slaughterhouse–meat markets continued to make the sausage, but that number dwindled as the number of custom slaughterhouses declined. Jenkins says slaughterhouses used to be everywhere in Louisiana. Now there are only about twenty in the state.

Bourgeois's sidelined its slaughter business several years ago. Lester Bourgeois, on one of his daily visits to the meat market, told me he missed it because there was tremendous gratification in doing the task correctly. When Bourgeois's still functioned as a slaughterhouse, Lester and Donald spent hours breaking down the carcasses of both livestock and game. Now, with its slaughterhouse shuttered, Bourgeois's buys state-inspected pork blood from a slaughterhouse ten miles north in the town of Chackbay.

There were two other commercial blood boudin makers besides Bourgeois's in the state and they were both in Acadiana, west of Baton Rouge. I made plans to visit them.

First on the list was C. Hebert's Slaughterhouse in low-lying Abbeville in Vermillion Parish. The town sits less than twenty miles north of sleepy marshes and wetlands, beyond which lie Vermillion Bay and the Gulf of Mexico. C. Hebert's is a stripped-down, all-business custom slaughterhouse that processes livestock for local families and deer for hunters. The retail counter sells cuts of meat and plenty of boudin.

But before I could get the words completely out about my research, owner Junior Luquette said he'd gotten tired of the inspection process and had stopped making blood boudin a couple of months earlier. "Too much trouble," said Junior crisply. "Just one of those things."

The only one remaining on my list was Babineaux's Slaughterhouse in Breaux Bridge, a Cajun town of about 8,100 that produces significant boudin per capita. Bob Carriker has reviewed eight purveyors here. Established in 1968, Babineaux's is run by brothers Rodney and Larry Babineaux in a cinderblock building off Highway 328. The place has weathered charm and is still going strong processing beef, pork, and venison and producing traditional *boudin blanc* and *noir*.

The range of boudin outlets in Breaux Bridge demonstrates the varying experiences available to anyone interested in the dish. Down the road from Babineaux's is Poché's, a large-scale Cajun meat market complete with a retail counter, mail-order business, and a restaurant serving plate lunches. Links of pork or crawfish boudin are retrieved from a pressure cooker near the cash register, just two items on a lengthy board of fare that includes several varieties of smoked pork sausage, andouille, tasso, the chorizo-like Cajun sausage, chaurice, and chaudin. Streams of customers pour into the store throughout the day, both from the local community and from Interstate-10, a few miles away.

If Poché's is the convivial, high-volume Cajun road food store, Babineaux's is an unadorned, straightforward abattoir focused on its main mission, meat processing. A single cold case at the front holds a few cuts of fresh meat, along with an aluminum tray of white and blood boudin.

It's hard to find a more authentic boudin-making operation than Babineaux's since the entire process starts with the slaughter of the pig. Once the animal is dispatched with an electric prod to the head, its carcass is hoisted high on a large meat hook in a room in the slaughterhouse called the kill floor. Rodney and Larry "catch" blood from the jugular vein of the pig using a funnel-like attachment that ensures the flow from the neck to a vessel is free of contamination. A state meat inspector from the Department of Agriculture has to be on hand to witness the draining process. The Babineauxs add an anticoagulant to the blood and refrigerate it for a day or two. It takes about three pigs to acquire the gallon and a half of blood necessary for a batch of their blood boudin.

After the slaughtered pig is thoroughly bled, the brothers and their workers use a mechanical arm to submerge the carcass by the hoof in a square-shaped pool of scalding water for about three minutes, which loosens its hair. Then they raise it from the bath and lay it onto a horizontal agitator. It shakes and bounces the carcass so dramatically it knocks off most of the hair; any remaining is removed by a blowtorch or shaved away with a large knife. As I'm watching this part of the operation, which feels a little like sitting through a campy slasher movie, I'm conflicted about whether to stare or look away.

When this step is complete, the denuded pig is laid out on a table, gutted, and its head removed. Then the carcass is ready to be broken down into individual cuts, including the pork shoulder and organ meats that Larry and Rodney use to make boudin.

Like Bourgeois's, Babineaux's cooks the meat slowly in a large stainless steel pot until tender and then separates it from the bone. They grind the meat and blend it with spices, minimal aromatic vegetables, and cooked rice. At this point, about half the pot's contents are loaded into the sausage maker and stuffed into natural pork casings to make white boudin. The brothers stir in the blood to the remaining boudin mixture, which turns it from ashen to scarlet. They fill the casings and steam the links. About half of the four to six hundred pounds of boudin that Babineaux's makes each week is blood boudin. If consumption has been dropping off in Louisiana, Rodney and Larry haven't noticed it. "Lots of people come from all over to get it," said Rodney in Breaux Bridge's distinct lilt. "We get a lot of calls, and not all from old people."

Still, blood boudin may ultimately be in peril even at this slaughterhouse. The brothers haven't yet figured out how to keep the operation going after they retire. It's a tough business to hand down or sell, they say, due to the high cost of insurance and the time it takes to meet regulatory requirements. Even with the possibility of boutique, grass-fed livestock creating new markets, the demand for custom slaughter doesn't come close to what it once was. The average consumer wants to go to the grocery store and buy one cut of meat at a time, the brothers tell me. Moreover, few families have the time, space, and inclination to raise livestock. "Used to be, everybody raised animals. More kids were in 4-H," says Larry, pointing at me with a blood-encrusted forefinger. "But why should they now? For one thing, it's expensive. And another, they have a pig and their neighbor complains, so they can't have the pig no more. They have cattle, but they figure it's too much trouble, so they sell their land and somebody puts up a subdivision."

He pauses, and adds, "There used to be three slaughterhouses just in Breaux Bridge. Now, we're one of the only ones out here."

Author's note: The brothers were right to be concerned about the challenges of keeping the establishment open into the next generation. Babineaux's Slaughterhouse closed in Spring 2014, after forty-six years of operation.

Boudin Balls with Two Dipping Sauces

One of boudin's most delicious by-products is boudin balls, and I don't miss a chance to pick some up when I'm near a Cajun butcher shop. I also like making them at home because you get the incomparable flavor of boudin in a format that's fairly easy to pull off. These delicious nuggets are fantastic party food. Order some casings, and use the filler to make your own boudin links as well.

As with so many other native Cajun and Creole recipes, you can put your own spin on this recipe by using different spices, playing around with the wet and dry batters, or adding pork liver (I left it out simply for convenience, and because liverless boudin is more common among purveyors near Baton Rouge, where I live). But one thing I highly recommend is starting with a bone-in pork shoulder (Boston Butt) prepared either by oven roasting with plenty of water in the pan, or by braising on the stove-top until it falls off the bone. The cut has plenty of fat and flavor, and the cooking methods ensure you have lots of broth—essential in binding the pork, rice, and aromatic veggies.

Makes 2 dozen.

> 2 ½ cups finely minced cooked pork butt (roasted or simmered), preferably warm
> 2 tablespoons olive oil
> 2 cups finely diced yellow onion
> 1 cup finely chopped green onions, white and green parts
> 4 cloves minced garlic
> 4 tablespoons chopped parsley
> 2 cups cooked medium-grain white rice
> 1 ½ cups defatted pork broth
> 1 ½ teaspoons kosher salt
> ¾ teaspoon black pepper

½ teaspoon cayenne pepper (increase to ¾ teaspoon or more if
    you prefer it hot)
Canola oil for frying
⅔ cup milk
2 eggs
½ cup panko bread crumbs
½ cup cracker meal or corn meal
1 teaspoon salt
½ teaspoon garlic powder
Spicy Mayhaw Dipping Sauce (recipe follows)
Garlic Chipotle Mayonnaise (recipe follows)

In a small skillet, heat olive oil over medium high heat and sauté the onion, green onions, and garlic until very soft, but not browned. Add the parsley and turn off the heat. Place pork, sautéed veggies, rice, pork broth, salt, black pepper, and cayenne pepper into a large mixing bowl and combine well.

Pour enough canola oil to reach 3 inches in a large, heavy pot and place over medium-high heat. Whisk milk and eggs together and set aside. In another bowl, combine panko bread crumbs, cracker meal, salt, and garlic powder.

Using your fingers, form the pork-rice mixture into golf ball–sized balls. Carefully roll each ball in wet batter, then dry batter, ensuring the dry batter is coated evenly on the surface. Place on a lined baking sheet until ready to cook. At this point, the boudin balls can be refrigerated or frozen, but bring to room temperature before frying.

When oil reaches 375 degrees F (use a candy or deep-fry thermometer), add boudin balls. If you don't have a thermometer, test one of the boudin balls. If the oil is hot enough it will cook perfectly in 2 minutes.

Using a slotted spoon, transfer fried balls to a baking sheet lined with paper towels. Serve hot or at room temperature with dipping sauces.

Spicy Mayhaw Dipping Sauce

Makes 1 cup.

½ cup mayhaw jelly
½ cup rice wine vinegar
1 tablespoon garlic chili paste

Combine jelly and vinegar in a small saucepan over medium heat, whisking until smooth. Whisk in garlic chili paste and serve.

Chipotle Mayonnaise

Makes 1 ½ cups.

1 cup mayonnaise
2 chipotle peppers in adobo sauce
¼ cup lime juice
¼ cup lemon juice
2 tablespoons chopped fresh parsley
2 tablespoons chopped fresh cilantro
2 tablespoons chopped fresh chives

Combine mayonnaise, peppers, lime juice, and lemon juice in a food processor and pulse until combined and smooth. Stir in herbs and serve.

7
Red Hot
Tamales

Shortly after we paid our admission fee at the ticket counter and crossed through a narrow gate into the fairgrounds, John and I could hear the noise. Top-40 music blared and the crowd began to cheer as seven young women took seats around a banquet table on the stage of an outdoor pavilion. One of them, LaRissa Faithe Phillips, seventeen, removed her seven-inch rhinestone tiara before sitting down. Two days earlier this group had been officially crowned the Zwolle Tamale Fiesta's Royal Court and were photographed in colorful Spanish ruffle dresses against a red and yellow bunting background. Now they were about to see who among them could polish off a dozen pork tamales first.

The announcer screamed, "Ready, go!" and the teens began unfurling tamales from their cornhusk jackets, sipping water between quick nibbles to help each mouthful slide down. Phillips, the year's Tamale Fiesta Queen, took an early lead, slapping the table in determination as she swallowed and sneaking a smiling glance at her competitors. Volunteers moved behind them and removed spent cornhusks and refilled plastic water cups. We festival goers watched expectantly, while the music pulsed and a warm breeze whipped around on the balmy October afternoon.

Before the song ended, Phillips's thin arm shot up and the crowd cheered. Her pile of tamales had vanished, making her the winner of the Royal Court's tamale-eating contest for the third consecutive year. Dressed in jeans, flat sandals, and a red festival t-shirt, she stood up confidently, replaced the tiara, and picked up a portable microphone to thank the crowd and resume her emcee responsibilities. There were subsequent tamale-eating contests to officiate onstage, and she needed to get back to work.

Since 1976, Zwolle (pronounced ZWAH-lee) has held an annual tamale festival to celebrate its signature dish. Tamales are made elsewhere in Louisiana, but no other city in the state does it like they do here in this small north Louisiana community of less than 1,800. Generations of mothers and grandmothers in Zwolle have passed down tamale recipes to their children—recipes that at one time relied on hand-ground corn and meat from boiled hogs' heads. The dish has probably been made in the area since the late eighteenth century. Today, tamales remain a mainstay of Zwolle family dinners, church suppers, and holiday parties. They're sold in convenience stores, by cottage industry tamale makers, at a local factory, and from the pickup trucks of mobile entrepreneurs. In Zwolle, charities raise money by selling tamales instead of doughnuts or raffle tickets.

More than four hours northwest of New Orleans and minutes from the Louisiana-Texas border, Zwolle feels like a remote outpost, especially to those of us coming from south Louisiana. When I mentioned my plan to visit Zwolle and attend its annual Tamale Fiesta to friends in Baton Rouge, many of them were unfamiliar with the city and its culinary event. I wasn't surprised. North and south Louisiana can feel like different worlds whose residents feel strong ties to their immediate surroundings. If I hadn't learned about Zwolle tamales years earlier from a friend who lived in nearby Natchitoches, I might not have known about Zwolle either.

Indeed, the town isn't easy to reach. The closest interstate, I-49, is forty miles to the east. Even if you're planning to visit the biggest attraction near Zwolle, the Toledo Bend reservoir, you're more likely to reach it by driving on Louisiana Highway 6, which doesn't pass through Zwolle at all.

Still, the town has managed to establish a cult following for its hallmark food, which is why the four-day festival attracts about ten thousand visitors every second weekend in October. During the rest of the year, travelers through the area sometimes detour through the town to purchase tamales from the E. B. Tamale Company, a family business founded in 1981 on the town's tumbledown main street. The factory, as locals call it, makes tamales and ships them throughout Louisiana, Arkansas, and Texas. Or if you know where to go, you can hit one of the small-batch home-based producers who still make tamales by hand using family recipes.

The festival got off the ground in 1976. Zwolle community leaders drew inspiration from celebrations marking the U.S. Bicentennial and created a local gathering intended to attract visitors and build tourism and community pride. By then, other small towns in Louisiana had successfully organized food festivals, and it seemed natural to organize an event in Zwolle around tamales. A local man named Rogers Loupe who taught agriculture and was a member of the Louisiana State Tourism advisory board is credited for the fiesta's founding. His son and daughter-in-law, Chris and Becky Loupe, continue to help organize the event every year.

Zwolle was founded in 1896 when a Dutch financier funded an extension of the railroad through the area and named the community for his hometown back in Holland. Zwolle's tamale tradition, however, started more than a century before when the region was part of New Spain. Spanish soldiers traveled back and forth between a settlement in Nacogdoches, Texas, to a fort and mission southeast of Zwolle called Los Adaes. The soldiers used a pathway called El Camino Real de los Tejas, the "king's highway" or "royal road." It later became Louisiana

State Highway 6. This was the primary overland route used by the Spanish to connect Mexico, the Rio Grande Valley in Texas, and Louisiana's Red River Valley. Tamales had originated in Mesoamerica thousands of years earlier, and Spanish soldiers became acquainted with them after the conquest and establishment of New Spain. As they traveled throughout the expansive territory, they brought along tamales, a convenient, portable food replicable from place to place. Its two main ingredients were corn and a source of protein, usually wild game.

Los Adaes closed in 1772, but many of the soldiers who served the fort remained in the area, some intermarrying with Native American tribes and setting up households in and around Zwolle. A large number of modern families in Zwolle trace their roots to these original Spanish settlers. In fact, the town's ethnic diversity is one of its defining features and something its residents often point out. Most Zwolle natives claim one of three principal ancestries: Spanish, African, or Native American. Some residents claim a tri-racial ethnicity.

Zwolle's early history took an interesting twist after the United States purchased the Louisiana Territory from the French in 1803. A dispute broke out between the Americans and the Spanish about the location of the territory's western boundary, the area that began north of Zwolle and ran south to the Gulf of Mexico. The two nations couldn't agree, so the land, called the "Neutral Strip," was ungoverned between 1806 and 1822. It attracted those on the lam, including freed and escaped slaves, criminals who were known to prey on travelers, and anyone else who wanted to live outside the law. Jean Lafitte, the privateer and slave trader, is believed to have operated for several years in the Neutral Strip. The boundary quarrel was resolved in 1822, but the north-south strip remained somewhat isolated for the rest of the century. The seclusion bred a kind of Wild West philosophy in the area that lasted into the twentieth century.

Modern Zwolle began to grow and prosper as a logging and oil and gas community, but it was known for lawlessness and violence. Quinton Brandon was a city marshal in Zwolle after World War II, earning the nickname "the marshal who tamed Zwolle" for his efforts to quell the crime rate. "It was dangerous back then," his daughter Becky Loupe told me on one of my research trips to Zwolle. "If you were a woman, you'd never walk alone in town."

Even into the twenty-first century, Zwolle has had a difficult time losing its reputation. Loupe's niece, Quinn Bowermeister, a graduate of Zwolle High School and former high school softball player, says that she and her teammates were frequently asked by opposing teams if they were armed. "The running joke in the other towns around here is that if you go to Zwolle, you better have a knife or a gun," she says.

Local leaders have worked hard to shift the focus to something positive, namely Zwolle's unique culinary history. The festival became an important event to the community because it celebrated a beloved dish that brought families together and that wasn't made quite the same elsewhere.

Ask Zwolle residents about tamales, and they're quick to point out that theirs are different from others around the country because they fuse Spanish and Native American culinary traditions. These tamales are smaller and spicier than those found in the American southwest and in Tex-Mex restaurants. In contrast to the famed tamales from the Mississippi Delta, they are not sauced with grease-tinged steaming liquid, smothered in chili, or served with soda crackers. And unlike the popular Mickey Brown wax-paper-wrapped beef tamales of Houma, Louisiana, Zwolle tamales are almost always made with pork, and each one is tucked in softened cornhusk referred to here as a "shuck."

Adjacent to the pavilion where the tamale-eating contests continue, longtime Zwolle resident Ethel Diener is holding a tamale-making demonstration under a red and white festival tent. Behind her, temporary latticework is draped in blue bunting and straw sombreros. She waits as a small crowd gathers, her hands resting comfortably on a table that holds a neat arrangement of ingredients: a plastic container of corn husks, an aluminum bowl of spiced ground pork, another bowl holding pasty cornmeal dough, shakers of cayenne pepper, black pepper, garlic powder, a carton of salt, a sack of *masa harina* (the corn flour used for tortillas and tamales), and three glass jars of corn kernels.

"We make more of an Indian tamale here," Ethel says to her audience. "I'm going to show you the long way, the way everybody around here used to make them and some people still do." Each jar shows corn kernels in different stage of softening, demonstrating how Zwolle towns people used to boil corn with the alkaline compound lime (calcium hydroxide), which has been used extensively throughout the world for a variety of purposes, culinary and non-culinary. Referred to scientifically as nixtamalization, the process has been documented in the ancient culinary practices of Mesoamerica. It was also recorded at Los Adaes by the French traveler Pierre Marie Francois de Pages, who wrote in his journal about Spanish settlers subsisting on corn, using lime to soften it, forming it into a pasty dough, and cooking the corn cakes over an open fire. At the site of Los Adaes, Louisiana state archaeologists have collected pieces of *metates* and *manos*, the mealing stone and hand tool used to grind corn, which Spanish settlers likely brought from the southern reaches of New Spain.

The thought of boiling corn in a chemical compound descends upon the crowd. "Lime?" a woman from Baton Rouge asks. Ethel responds, "Yes. You have to wash it real good after that. About eleven times." Indeed, eleven rinses are the prescribed amount in the town's official tamale recipe, although locals concede the goal is simply to make sure the water rinses clear. Most home cooks circumvent this step by using masa harina, a meal made from corn that has already been nixtamalized, to make their dough instead.

Ethel picks up a cornhusk and lays it flat on her left palm. Then she grabs a few tablespoons of the cornmeal mixture and, with her fingertips in a tight bunch, she spreads it evenly across the center of the husk. She calls this "daubing." When she has tapped the dough into a flat circle inside the husk, she gently spreads a teaspoon or two of the spiced, cooked pork mixture down the center. Pork shoulder and pork trimmings are the primary cuts of meat used in today's Zwolle tamales, replacing the hog's head of yesteryear. As she talks, she rolls the husk like a cigar and then folds one end over, sealing it off. The other end is left open. She then explains the process of positioning the tamales upright in a saucepan, folded side down, and steaming them gently until the cornmeal cooks through.

Not far from Ethel's demonstration, a red and white banner on the town's multi-purpose building advertises *Zwolle Tamales Sold Here,* and festival patrons are in line at a service window. The tamales are made by the E. B. Tamale Company, founded in 1981 by Zwolle entrepreneur and real estate developer E. B. Malmay and his son Larry, and run today by Malmay's daughter Ginger Box and her husband Bernie. John and I join the line.

In the warm fall sun, patrons patiently wait to exchange cash for plastic grocery bags holding tamales by the dozen, five thousand of which will be sold by the end of the weekend. It may be possible to buy tamales in threes or sixes in the Mississippi Delta, but in Zwolle a dozen is standard. Hungry customers take a seat at one of several folding tables under the pavilion or they spread out on the grass, as we do, and begin opening their aluminum foil–wrapped bundles.

An arm-wrestling competition ensues on stage, and children squeal from carnival rides in an adjacent field. A group of men discuss Zwolle High School's upcoming basketball season. Football is unquestionably the dominant sport in Louisiana thanks to the long shadow cast by the LSU Tigers and the New Orleans Saints, but here, basketball is king. The Zwolle Hawks have won multiple Class B high school state championships in the last few decades, earning themselves the spirited but ethnically flawed nickname the Cajun Hoosiers. Like tamales, basketball is another point of pride for the community.

Families and friends sit together and unwrap a succession of tamales. John and I dig into our own and savor their tender, moist texture. They're not particularly greasy, nor are they overstuffed. The cornmeal crust is toothsome and pliable. It's sturdy enough to hold upright before taking a bite. The ground pork inside is assertively spiced with cayenne and red pepper flakes, but not perilously so. You won't find chili powder or cumin in Zwolle tamales, or anything else that might overpower its two primary ingredients, pork and cornmeal. The dish is an exercise in precision and restraint, and each of our tamales disappears in a few bites.

A few months before the festival, I had come to Zwolle to visit Bernie and Ginger Box at their main street tamale company. The Boxes never anticipated taking over Ginger's dad's tamale business. They had lived and raised their children in Shreveport, an hour north, where Bernie had worked as an engineer and Ginger as an accountant. But after her father died in 2000, Ginger began returning to Zwolle periodically to help keep the factory running. Her brother Larry had been killed in a car accident several years earlier, making her the logical successor. The business was more demanding than they'd anticipated, so with their own children out of the house, she and Bernie eventually found themselves in Zwolle, living in her family home and making tamales full-time.

The company churns out about 3,500 dozen tamales a week and ships them to stores in the region; they are stamped with the label "The Original Zwolle Tamale." While the Boxes and I are visiting, the glass doors swing open and slam shut loudly. It's a young salesman passing through town and he wants to buy a dozen spicy. A few minutes later the phone rings, but the Boxes let it go to voicemail. I hear a woman leaving a relieved message about ordering tamales for her mother, who now lives in Florida. *I finally found you. She's driving me crazy about your tamales. Please call me.*

"The other commercial tamales out there, they're nothing like ours," Ginger tells me. "They have too much spice or they come with sauce. Our tamales are different. You just don't find this type anywhere."

Tamales are neither a quick nor an easy dish to make. Here at the plant, with the help of commercial equipment, the process still takes place over three days. It begins with the preparation of the pork. The Boxes cook down pork trimmings in three large commercial stainless steel pots; then they grind the meat and add a signature dry spice mixture that includes black pepper, cayenne pepper, salt, paprika, and garlic powder.

On the second day, Ginger and Bernie boil dried kernels of corn and send them through a grinder as well. To the cornmeal, they add salt, broth, and lard to form dough. And on the third day, they load the dough and pork mixtures into separate chambers of a commercial extruder. The machine combines the two ingredients into a cylinder of cornmeal-wrapped pork, which emerges as a long, skinny unit before a sharp, rotating wheel cuts it into uniform 1.4-ounce pieces. Workers slide the individual tamales onto trays and hand-roll them into softened corn husks. The finished tamales are packaged by the dozen. Some are frozen for shipping; others are wrapped in aluminum foil for weekday sales here at the factory.

Ginger remembers making tamales as a child with her grandmother. "We would make them for the holidays," she reminisces. "You'd spend all day making several dozen. It's a big mess and it would take forever. Then they would be gone in no time."

~❧~

At the tamale demonstration, John and I listen as Ethel tells the crowd that you can tell whether a tamale has been rolled by hand or rolled with an extruder by the way it emerges from its husk. With a machine, the tamale is made first and then wrapped up in the shuck, so it comes out intact. But in a hand-rolled tamale, the shuck and the dough are rolled together, and you have to gently separate one from the other.

As Ethel talks, her close friend Judy Garcia looks on. Judy is a lifelong resident of Zwolle and one of the town's home-based tamale makers. Her husband, Stan, a retired retail store manager, is milling about the crowd, greeting friends and shaking hands while wearing a red and silver imperial crown. He's this year's Tamale Fiesta King.

Judy has been making tamales in earnest since the early 1970s, when her mother and stepfather bought a convenience store on Highway 171 North, once the only route from Zwolle to Shreveport. The family made and sold tamales there. After they sold the store, Judy continued making tamales to order from her home kitchen.

Her process begins on Sundays when she cooks down pork trimmings. "I don't season it while I'm cooking it," she tells me. "When I grind the meat, that's when I put the seasonings in." She uses paprika, red pepper flakes, cayenne pepper, and salt.

By Tuesday the meat portion of the dish is prepared, and she begins work on the dough, combining *masa,* warm water, and broth and fat from the cooked pork. "You know the dough is right when you daub it on your hand and it peels right off," she says. "If it sticks to your hand, you know it's going to stick to the shuck." She uses a small extruder to assemble the tamales, wraps them in shucks, and steams them in a large pot. Judy makes tamales with four different levels of spiciness, which she calls mild, medium, extra hot, and "souped up" hot.

The annual festival weekend results in an uptick in tamale orders for Judy and the other tamale producers in town. Frank's Tamales, which still makes tamale dough by grinding corn, supplies the tamales for the festival's kick-off supper. The L&W Tamale House, Sepulvado's Country Tamales, and other small businesses fill large numbers of orders for families who gather over the weekend. A lot of people hold family reunions during the fiesta. It's a good reason to come back home.

As the afternoon progresses, the crowds meander past booths where vendors sell homemade candles, polished quartz crystals, and pine-cone Christmas wreaths. The midway whirs and clangs with kiddie rides and games of chance. A couple of dozen food booths offer requisite carny fare—funnel cakes, chicken-on-a-stick, and "Texas tater tornados," deep-fried whole potatoes cut to resemble misshapen chrysanthemums.

A short walk from the heart of the festival is a large tract of open land where the mud bog takes place, a huge draw that attracts regional aficionados of the off-road sport. Fairgoers position chairs along twin one-hundred-yard mud trenches, through which contestants will attempt to drive vehicles at top speeds without flipping over or stalling engines. Queen LaRissa Phillips and two members of her royal court are there to open the event, after which the crowd sings the National Anthem, ball caps removed deferentially and children silenced. A cheer goes up after the anthem ends, and then jacked-up cars and trucks with names like "Let's Get Nasty" and "Never Satisfied" take their marks. One by one, they fire their massive engines and hurl themselves through the channel, while spectators cheer and mud flies. We're fifty yards away from the nearest truck, but a wet nugget of mud still manages to land on the surface of my sunglasses.

Later in the day back on Main Street, the town begins to quiet as locals file to their cars and return home to family gatherings. Day-trippers like us head for the state highway with take-home bags of tamales. The images of the bullfighter and the sombrero-topped cacti that adorn the plate-glass windows of the downtown Western Auto store will soon be wiped away—painted again this time next year.

When the tamale festival first took place back in 1976, it repelled Zwolle's older residents, who believed it poked fun at the town's Spanish-Indian heritage. As Becky Loupe recalls, "A lot of them stayed home that first year, but when they saw that it was a real celebration of what we have, they came out and supported it. The fiesta has grown and grown every year beyond our imagination. To me, it says a lot about our little town."

The Official Zwolle Tamale Recipe

One of the attractions of the annual Zwolle Tamale Fiesta is a tamale-making demonstration by local residents, who are proud to show how Zwolle tamales were once made. They distribute the "Official Zwolle Tamale Recipe," a formula that is also featured in the town's 2011 cookbook, *Second Helping of Sharing Our Best*. I have modified this recipe slightly from the original, in an attempt to provide specific measurements where there were none. Otherwise, it remains preserved. It belonged to a Zwolle resident named Pauline Longoria, who won the festival's tamale-making contest during its inaugural year.

Makes 30 dozen.

> 10-pound pork roast (originally, meat from 1 ½ hog heads
>   was used)
> Water
> 3 cloves garlic, peeled and chopped
> 1 cup plus 3 tablespoons lard
> 2 tablespoons salt
> 2 teaspoons cayenne pepper
> 2 teaspoons black pepper
> 1 gallon yellow corn kernels
> ½ cup pickling lime
> 30 dozen corn shucks

Day One

Place pork roast in a large stock pot, add enough cold water to cover, and bring to boil. Simmer for about 2 hours or until meat is tender. Cool. Remove meat from pot, reserving broth. Debone meat thoroughly and chop fine or run through a meat grinder.

Sauté garlic in three tablespoons of lard and add to ground pork. Add salt, cayenne pepper, and black pepper. Adjust seasonings depending on preference for hot, medium, or lightly seasoned tamales.

Boil corn kernels in water with lime in a large pot until they becomes tender, about 1 hour. Rinse and drain corn with cold water 11 times to remove lime. Place kernels in containers or bags in freezer for 4–6 hours before grinding.

Day Two

Grind corn. Mix with remaining 1 cup lard and pork broth. Salt to taste. Test dough on palm of hand. If dough is pliable, it is ready. If not, add more lard.

Wash corn shucks and soak them in scalding water. Remove one shuck at a time from water, dry, and flatten on palm of hand. With other hand, daub a few teaspoons of corn mixture onto shuck, spreading it cross-wise to both edges, leaving both ends of the shuck free of dough. Spread a heaping teaspoon of the meat mixture lengthwise over the dough. Roll shuck lengthwise and fold one end over about 2 inches.

Stand tamales with folded ends down into a large stove-top steamer until steamer is completely packed. Pour in about 3 inches of water, but do not let it cover the tamales. Cover tightly and cook on low for about an hour and a half.

Tamales can be frozen and reheated by placing them in a rice cooker or steamer until warm.

8

A Strong Attachment
Oysters

Louisiana's serpentine coastline is a miraculous place. Its picturesque inlets and estuaries are among the most fertile on the planet, spawning multitudes of fish, mollusks, and crustaceans and supporting a range of other animal species. Fresh water from the Mississippi and Atchafalaya rivers flows through the state and tumbles past the coast into the Gulf of Mexico, creating ecosystems so rich in life they have helped Louisiana build a $2.4 billion seafood industry, one of the largest in the country. The creatures that thrive —oysters, shrimp, crab, and fish—are central components of Louisiana's menu, hallmarks of its culinary identity.

Among these gems, the oyster has an irresistible and compelling story, and I'm on my way to the wetlands south of the city of Houma to see it firsthand. Here off the coast, the oyster has thrived for centuries, snuggled against shells and other hard surfaces, patiently filtering nutrients. As it did in other locales across the globe, the creature sustained generations of indigenous peoples and immigrants because it was a perfect, compact protein, consumable on the spot. Forget the need for fire.

All that was, and still is, required to enjoy an oyster is a blunt tool and a steady hand.

Many of the signature ingredients in Cajun and Creole cuisine, including rice and okra, are non-native species that were introduced to the region by resourceful settlers. Not the oyster. It is Louisiana's original local food, a reliable staple that made an enduring impact on the state's culinary ethos.

Louisiana's love affair with oysters began more than three hundred years ago. Plentiful and accessible, they quickly became part of the diet of French immigrants who arrived in New Orleans and its environs at the beginning of the eighteenth century, as well as that of the Acadians who fled Nova Scotia and settled across south Louisiana after 1750. These groups found an endless supply of oysters nestled in the coastal zone. Around 1850, the relationship between the oyster and the people of Louisiana intensified when waves of Croatians who had fished and oystered in the Adriatic Sea established themselves southeast of New Orleans, largely in Plaquemines Parish. Laying the groundwork for the oyster industry we know today, these fishermen pioneered new equipment, including rake-like dredges they tossed from oyster boats, which were more efficient in harvesting oysters than commonly used tongs. The Croatian community also understood the need to replenish the reef and was the first to populate harvest beds with seed oysters, juveniles from elsewhere in the coastal zone.

By the turn of the twentieth century, state officials rightly recognized that Louisiana's abundant supply could form the basis of a powerful oyster industry. Lawmakers passed legislation in 1902 that helped accelerate oyster production in the state while also ensuring that supply wasn't depleted. Oyster fishing had formerly been monitored only at the parish level, but after 1902, the state centralized management and began issuing oyster leases directly to individual oystermen. This move helped the industry expand because each oysterman suddenly had a vested interest in his particular lease and began taking steps to make sure it was as productive as possible.

Thus, a typical oysterman made it his habit to toss half shells to the bayou's muddy floor to ensure there was enough hard material, or substrate, on which new generations of oysters could attach. During harvest, the fishers were also careful to throw back smaller, juvenile oysters to give them a chance to grow and propagate. The state helped oystermen further expand their oyster populations by allowing them to source seed oysters from public oyster grounds. Before long, Louisiana had an army of enterprising oyster farmers who were making money while acting as conservationists.

Meanwhile, the oyster's culinary appeal continued to grow in the United States and throughout south Louisiana. In 1889, Antoine's Restaurant in New Orleans introduced what arguably remains the world's most famous baked oyster dish: Oysters Rockefeller. By then, the French-Creole eatery in the city's French Quarter had been open for forty-nine years.

The legend goes something like this: Chef-owner Jules Alciatore had intended to use snails for a new dish, but a French snail shortage forced him to turn to oysters as the principal ingredient. He combined oysters with watercress or local greens and something that imparted an anise flavor, probably fresh fennel or absinthe, and placed the amalgam onto the empty half shell. To this day, Antoine's won't reveal its recipe, but numerous interpretations over the years have called for spinach, breadcrumbs, and an anise-flavored liqueur such as Herbsaint. Topped with rich white sauce and baked, the dish was named for Standard Oil magnate John D. Rockefeller, then one of the country's wealthiest men.

Oysters Rockefeller sparked a bevy of other baked-on-the-half-shell dishes, including the New Orleans–born Oysters Bienville, which involves draping the oysters in a white sauce with shrimp and grated parmesan cheese. *River Road Recipes,* the formidable community cookbook produced by the Junior League of Baton Rouge in 1959 and one of the best-selling cookbooks of its kind in the country, includes no fewer than eleven baked-oyster dishes. Seafood restaurants around Louisiana have developed plenty of other baked-oyster traditions over the years, including the famed herb and breadcrumb-topped Oysters Mosca at Mosca's Restaurant in Avondale outside of New Orleans. Also of regional note is Oysters Maxwell at Juban's Restaurant in Baton Rouge, which shellacs the oyster in mozzarella cheese, bacon, cocktail sauce, and jalapenos.

There's no shortage of other oyster applications in Louisiana, especially in the southern half of the state, where restaurants are awash in charbroiled oysters and oyster po'boys. New Orleans is famous for these oyster dishes as well as for the home-grown oyster loaf—a hollowed-out baton of French bread stuffed with deep-fried oysters. Across Louisiana kitchens, oysters and artichokes are a classic combination, both in soup and in a casserole. Holiday tables regularly include scalloped oysters or oyster dressing alongside pans of cornbread or rice dressing. And, of course, there is the enduring tradition of raw bars, where deft shuckers pry open shells by inserting stubby knives into a sweet spot near the hinge. Onto a tray of ice the oysters go, to be slurped down unadorned or with a douse of hot sauce, a smidge of horseradish, and a saltine cracker.

On a clear 60-degree January morning—the peak of the regional oyster season—I'm headed to Bayou Dularge with Jason Gilfour, the corporate chef at a major oyster processor in Houma called Motivatit Seafood. The century-old business processes between forty thousand and sixty thousand pounds of oysters a day, all extracted from the coastal waters here in the southeast part of the state—waterways that include Bayou Dularge. The bayou is located about ten miles into the wetlands due south of Houma, a city of about thirty thousand in southern Terrebonne Parish. Jason and I are meeting Motivatit's farm manager and Jason's brother-in-law, Jarod Voisin, who keeps an eye on the thousands of acres of oyster beds the company leases off the coast. A bevy of contract oystermen fish the beds, transporting hundreds of burlap sacks crammed with mud-laced oysters back to the plant every day.

Before heading out to the bayou, Jason takes me around the Motivatit plant, a marvel of ingenuity. The oyster industry is a study in extremes. On one end is the small, generational fisherman accustomed to eking out a living. He lives on the margins and feels the blow of natural—and manmade—disasters sharply. On the other is the large-scale player who has built a sizable operation and has helped position the state industry to compete nationally. Motivatit falls into the latter camp. Until his untimely death in January 2013, company CEO Mike Voisin, Jason's father-in-law, had helped expand this family business's bottom line while also shaping Louisiana's seafood public policy. Among other major accomplishments, Voisin helped pioneer the practice of dividing the state's coastline into numbered subsections, called areas, for the purpose of isolating potentially harmful incidents. If something necessitated the shutdown of one area, such as an environmental spill or the rare presence of the bacteria harmful to humans, *vibrio vulnificus*, then the entire coastline didn't have to arrest operations. Voisin, a beloved industry figure, believed that it was possible to be both safe and wildly productive. The conviction was in his bones: his father, Ernest, had developed technology that kills bacteria in an oyster through hydrostatic pressure, enabling the company to build a nationwide following for its Gold Band oysters. High pressure, as well as pasteurization, are the two main methods Gulf oyster producers have mitigated concerns about bacteria, especially during warmer months. As Jason and I stroll through into this portion of the plant, he picks up an oyster from a conveyer belt. It has just emerged from the pressure chamber. Its shell is opened slightly—one of the convenient by-products of the process. Jason opens it fully and hands it to me to taste. The oyster has a nice wiggly texture, but it's void of flavor. I'm anxious to pluck one from the wild instead.

We take a look at a few more of the plant functions, including assembly lines where choice oysters fresh from the high-pressured chambers are kept on their half shells and vacuum sealed for shipment to inland restaurants throughout the country. Louisiana oyster lovers, spoiled by the briny bounty of the coastal zone, would thumb their noses at frozen plastic packages of oysters on the half shell, but Motivatit deserves credit for broadening the market for Louisiana oysters. Plentiful and mild-tasting, oysters from the Pelican State have become the workhorse of the American oyster world and the ones most likely to land on plates outside of the state. More than 60 percent of the creatures harvested here are exported, many headed for cruise ships, casinos, and chain seafood restaurants. With two million acres of oyster beds that span the coast and about $350 million in annual revenue, Louisiana's oyster industry is the largest in the United States.

But enough business; it's time to head down the bayou, as locals say in this part of the state.

Jason and I hop into his SUV and hit the nearest highway headed south. Houma's mid-morning bustle soon gives way to a series of quiet fishing communities on the outskirts of town, a few of which the Voisins' ancestors emigrated to in the mid-eighteenth century during *Le Grande Dérangement*. We pass houses that sit on tall stilts—a post–Hurricane Katrina building requirement imposed by insurance companies in low-lying areas like this one. The area becomes increasingly rural with each passing mile, and it's hard not to notice a sharp polarization of income levels. Plots of land featuring new brick-and-stucco suburban-style houses are sprinkled among raggedy mobile homes and gone-to-seed cottages. Some homesteads are long abandoned and overgrown with scrub brush and weeds. Stately live oaks are frequent, their spidery limbs outstretched and draped in Spanish moss. Soon, the bayou appears on my right out of the passenger window, and I spot docked oyster and shrimp boats, bobbing gently against their moorings.

The boats are docked, Jason tells me, because many smaller oystermen aren't going out with the frequency they used to do. There is no question that Louisiana has spent the last century crafting a thriving oyster industry even as other parts of the United States, namely the Chesapeake Bay, saw theirs plummet because of pollution and aggressive harvesting. But Bayou State oystermen have had to endure natural and manmade threats to their livelihood, especially in recent memory.

Jason and I talk about the peculiar life of the average oysterman as we pass several slips where oyster boats without pilots sit in wait. Between 2005 and 2012 alone, an unusual number of challenges were visited upon the Louisiana coast in rapid succession, including five major hurricanes, an oil spill, and the continuing issue of coastal erosion. Hurricanes have always been drawn to the Gulf Coast, but the number of major storms that Louisiana has sustained recently is something new. And while storms are tough on Louisiana's entire seafood industry, they are particularly difficult for oystermen because of the pokey maturation process of the creatures themselves. Oysters make us wait.

It takes about two years for oysters to be ready for commercial harvest, and that is under good conditions. It's far tougher with back-to-back storms.

The damage results from a hurricane's storm surge, which sends a crushing wall of water against the fragile coast where oysters cluster. The force churns up mud and debris, smothering and choking off habitats. In August 2005, Hurricane Katrina roared into oyster-rich Plaquemines Parish south of New Orleans, wreaking havoc on oyster beds there. That disaster was followed by Hurricane Rita just one month later on the state's west side. Rita caused serious damage to the coastal zone south of Lake Charles, but the storm also sent floodwaters racing back to the state's eastern flank, adding to the damage caused by Katrina. Hurricane Gustav hit three years later in 2008, just as many of the beds had recovered, making landfall in the Terrebonne Parish fishing village of Cocodrie. One week later, Hurricane Ike made landfall in Galveston Bay, Texas, and sent a violent storm surge across the entire Louisiana coast.

Hurricanes aren't the only threat to oyster beds. In 2010, the British Petroleum offshore oilrig Deepwater Horizon exploded, releasing a torrent of oil into the Gulf. State officials responded by temporarily shutting down commercial fishing while biologists and water-quality experts immediately began testing waterways. The leak took months to seal permanently, and as oil threatened to creep from the Gulf into the wetlands, Louisiana governor Bobby Jindal ordered a fresh-water diversion to help flush the ecosystem. The initiative had the unintended and tragic consequence of killing large numbers of oyster beds, taking out as much as 98 percent of the oyster population in certain areas because of the abrupt change in salinity.

Meanwhile, coastal erosion has continued to affect the oyster industry. After the Great Mississippi River Flood of 1927, during which the river broke free from its levees and caused major destruction throughout its floodplain, Congress passed the Flood Control Act of 1928. Consequently, the U.S. Army Corps of Engineers began a herculean effort to harness the courses of the Mississippi and Atchafalaya rivers, creating a sophisticated system of levees, spillways, and flood-control measures in Louisiana. Changing the course of the rivers caused a massive shift in where they naturally deposited sediment. Formerly, the Mississippi had helped the wetlands maintain landmass because it naturally deposited silt on its way to the Gulf of Mexico. But after the river course was altered, the level of silt decreased dramatically. Moreover, in the 1930s, serious oil exploration began off the Louisiana coast, further altering the coastal zone. Oil companies perforated the marshes with an extensive network of pipelines and transportation channels. The new waterways allowed oil to be transported to the mainland and helped build a crucial domestic energy supply, but they forever changed the balance of salt and fresh water that the oyster requires. Like the diversion projects, these exploratory canals also sped up coastal erosion.

Consequently, Louisiana saw a 25 percent decrease in land area between 1932 and 2010, a loss of about 1,883 square miles, according to the U.S. Geological Survey. More than 16.5 miles of land along the coast have disappeared each year. We here in Louisiana have become too used to saying this rate equals the size of a football field lost every hour. The coastal zone is home to more than half of the state population. Of concern to the nation as a whole is that about 25 percent of the U.S.'s domestic oil supply comes from offshore Louisiana.

As we continue down the highway toward Jarod's boat landing, I watch a great blue heron take off from a passing dock. It flaps its wings so slowly and deliberately that I wonder how it remains aloft. I ask Jason how the people of the bayou region feel about the loss of landmass here and whether or not they think authorities will ever successfully stop it. This is a notoriously clannish part of Louisiana, an isolated nook in the state's southern reaches whose people are naturally suspicious of decision-makers from Baton Rouge and New Orleans. "Folks around here have just gotten immune to the discussion," he says. "They can see things changing in front of them, they see the land loss, but they can't believe anything will slow it down, and they have no plans to go anywhere else."

Indeed, state officials have discussed strategies for addressing the problem of the diminishing wetlands *ad nauseum*, but nothing has yet arrested the disturbing pace. Some momentum might have finally arrived, however. In 2012, the Louisiana legislature unanimously approved an extensively researched fifty-year coastal master plan, and British Petroleum agreed to pay out $42 billion to Gulf Coast states for damages and economic loss sustained after the oil spill. In Louisiana, some of those damage payments were assigned to the execution of various aspects of the master plan, including new controlled diversions that will send fresh water from the Mississippi and Atchafalaya rivers into the coastal wetlands. These diversions will dump badly needed silt and sediment in the wetlands as the rivers head to the Gulf. It's one of the best remedies for replenishing the eroding marsh, but its delivery device—fresh water—places some current oyster beds in peril.

꩜

We approach a small marina, pull into its gravel parking lot, and walk to a slip where Jarod, a beefy, fair-haired young man awaits with one of the boats he uses for scouting the company's beds.

We board the boat and Jarod pilots us away from the slip. There are bayous all over Louisiana, a porous state where sleepy, soggy waterways wind through even large cities. But bayous like this one are different. Decades of coastal erosion have chewed away at the land, leaving a veritable river interrupted by patches of marsh grass. The boat picks up speed, and the marina and mainland become distant specks as we head into Bayou Dularge. Egrets, herons, and a few roseate spoonbills wait patiently in the marshes, maneuvering their spindly legs from one point to the next and peering at the smooth surface for darting fish. From time to time, I can see a litter of oysters huddled against hard outcroppings in the marsh. For the most part, though, they live out of sight on the water bottom, undetectable until they're brought to the surface with the dredges that exist on every Louisiana oyster boat. They are the sole method of harvesting oysters in the state currently.

We laugh about the fact that Jarod, an eighth-generation oysterman, doesn't like the taste of oysters. It emerges when I ask him his favorite way to eat them. "No, ma'am," he tells me. "I don't like them. Never have." The sky is a cloudless blue, the air is crisp, and the water, glassy; it seems unfathomable that the wetlands are slowly being washed away. Will they, I wonder, be as resilient as the oyster? For millions of years in habitats like this one and others, the docile creature has pursued its odd life. There it sits, affixed to a hard surface, minding its affairs and unruffled by daily tumult. Its estuarial friends are in constant motion, but the oyster keeps perfectly still, filtering nutrients from the moving water, expelling tiny bubbles, and plumping up until it is time to release a dramatic blast of sperm and eggs into the water column. These free-floating gametes find each other, connect, and thousands of baby oysters begin their journeys. In the Gulf, this happens not once a year, as it does in most of the rest of the world, but twice, once in the spring and again in the fall.

For about two weeks, the babies float precariously in the water as small larvae, and many of them are consumed by tiny fish. The lucky ones use a freshly sprouted apparatus to maneuver to the bottom of the bayou, where their evolutionary memory tells them to grab onto a hard, clean surface—usually another oyster shell or manmade material placed there to help them along. Now known as oyster spat, these organisms sit and begin the process of growing two protective half shells, and they start to filter the nutrients that will fatten them up. They spawn and fatten and spawn again, fully mature and ready to eat in about two years. Barring hurricanes and predators, an oyster will sit undisturbed until a hardworking Louisiana oysterman slows his boat on the surface above and lowers a dredge into the water. The rake-like tool lodges on the muddy bottom, and the oysterman drags it along until it hits a patch of the bivalves. They're scraped from their perches, raised up from the water by the dredge, and dumped onto the boat's sorting table. The oysterman categorizes them by gloved hand, keeping those that measure three to six inches across and tossing back the smaller ones. The keepers are shoveled into burlap sacks and refrigerated on board. On a good day, the oysterman fills 50 to 100 sacks that weigh between 100 and 125 pounds each. By quitting time, he will deliver his catch to processors like Motivatit, who sort and ship it to seafood markets, grocery stores, oyster bars, restaurants, and food distributors in Louisiana and around the country.

Oyster farmers gain access to the water bottom by maintaining oyster leases, and they designate the location of these leases with marker buoys. Jarod spots the marker buoy he's looking for and slows the boat. The water laps gently against the craft's aluminum side as Jason picks up the manual dredge and heaves it into the water off the stern, letting it sink to the bottom. On a regular oyster boat, this process takes place with the help of a mechanical arm, but our boat is a smaller vessel, a scout boat used for assessing the productivity of the company's oyster acreage.

Jason hauls the dredge back into the boat, but it has extracted only sediment and debris. He tries again, casting the rake at a different spot. This time, the loose muck is joined by a dozen or so oysters of various sizes, so Jason pulls the dredge in and lets the oysters tumble onto the work surface. He reaches into his blue jeans back pocket for an oyster knife, sliding the blade in at the hinge and wedging the shells apart. The oyster sits on one of them, pale gray, glistening, and spewing a tiny bubble. He hands it to me. It's a pretty big one, and I fleetingly consider what I'll look like to these two strangers as I slurp down a naked, quivering oyster too large to fit in my mouth. Here goes. With my fingertip, I loosen the eye muscle that holds the oyster fast to the shell's slick wall and hold the whole thing in front of my lips. It feels like an industrial-sized serving spoon. Still, I tilt my head back and slurp, and I feel the oyster land on my tongue. I chew slightly and take in the flavor. The mild, sweet-salty meat tastes of nature itself. It's delicious. Jason cracks one open for himself. He eats them routinely, but this afternoon, he also can't deny that what we're feasting on is something special—a food steeped by the wind, waves, sediment, and nutrients that form and define the Louisiana coast.

A multitude of factors affects the overall taste of an oyster, from the composition and salinity of its waters to the surrounding microclimate to the topography of the shore, and plenty of oyster lovers are quick to claim that their particular region of the world produces the best ones. I've heard as much from friends and family who spend time in Apalachicola, Florida, and insist their oysters taste best. And especially along the East Coast, legacy oyster varieties like Wellfleet and Blue Point carry serious name recognition. My grandmother, a Baltimore native who relocated to Georgia in her late twenties after marrying my grandfather, was loath to give up the claim that the Chesapeake Bay produced the best oysters, often reminiscing about the sacks of fresh oysters delivered to her family basement and the anticipation they brought as they audibly "breathed" through their shells. But as much as oyster lovers in such locales hate to admit it, oysters up and down the eastern seaboard and throughout the Gulf of Mexico are part of the same species as those that hail from Louisiana, *Crassostrea virginica*. It's a point Jason and I laugh about. *C. virginica*, sometimes called the Eastern, American, or Atlantic oyster, is one of only two species that naturally occur in North America.

The other species, *Crassostrea gigas*, is found on the Pacific Coast. There might be distinctions in size, shape, and flavor in oysters from Galveston Bay to Bayou Dularge to Prince Edward Island, but their taxonomy is one and the same.

Against this backdrop, the relationship between the Gulf Coast oyster eater and her beloved bivalve is distinct. Elsewhere, the oyster is a pricy proposition; but off the coasts of Texas, Louisiana, Mississippi, Alabama, and Florida, it is plentiful and inexpensive. At the same time that East Coast oysters from the Long Island Sound or Martha's Vineyard are fetching $3 an oyster in mahogany-trimmed bars, the Gulf oyster is a twenty-five-cent happy-hour special accompanied by pitchers of cheap beer. On the East and West coasts, the oyster is precious and treated with a light hand, served raw or just barely poached in mignonette. In Louisiana in particular, it's wantonly tossed into gumbos, stews, and bisques, baked with rich toppings, wrapped with bacon, charbroiled with butter, deep-fried and dragged in cocktail sauce, tucked in po'boys, served in casseroles and holiday dressings, and gulped as a cocktail shooter.

Most ironic is that because the East Coast has seen its oyster population diminish so drastically over the course of the twentieth century, farmers there often turn to the Gulf for help. Many in the East Coast oystering world seed their beds with plentiful, juvenile Gulf oysters. "Finished" in northern waters, their Gulf Coast bloodline is buried and forgotten, and the oysters are sold with mid-Atlantic or northern pedigrees at sharply higher prices.

The supply of oysters from the Louisiana coast has been erratic since 2010, as some beds recover from the post-spill fresh water diversion and others fail to bounce back. In early 2013, a wildly productive area east of the Mississippi River called Breton Sound saw a sharp and inexplicable decline in its oyster population, and oyster biologists with the State of Louisiana's Department of Natural Resources were concerned. There seemed to be big problems with reproduction—few young oysters were spotted—and it made the harvest in the area's public grounds one of the worst on record.

All the same, the challenges that have been befallen the industry in recent years seem to have forced innovation. Oyster biologists, state officials, and the oyster industry itself have all backed a method of growing and harvesting oysters in Louisiana known as off-bottom culturing, a technique used in Australia, Japan, and elsewhere in the world as well, in which oysters are grown in baskets on lines suspended in the water. This approach keeps the oysters safe from predators and allows oystermen to select areas less prone to natural disaster and changes in salinity. The shift to this method was a radical step in Louisiana, where oysters have been harvested exclusively from the water bottom since the industry's beginning.

Research underway at the LSU Sea Grant Oyster Hatchery in Grand Isle since 2002 is designed to perfect the use of off-bottom culturing to supplement the common on-bottom approach. The hatchery has been experimenting with a system developed in Australia, in which oysters grow suspended in three-foot-long mesh baskets that are hung from horizontal cables and suspended just under the surface of the water. The method is promising for a number of reasons. It shortens the average life cycle of an oyster from two years to about twelve to sixteen months. This "cage" method is also less labor intensive, since oysters are harvested from the same baskets they're grown in. And it keeps oysters from being buried in silt and mud during weather events. In 2012, the Louisiana legislature approved a bill allowing the industry to use off-bottom culture methods; until then, on-bottom was the only method allowed.

Incorporating a new method of harvest won't be easy, since all aspects of the industry, from boat equipment to oyster leases, have been based on on-bottom harvest. But oyster leaders believe the state's industry must evolve and that a dual approach will protect the harvest in the future. Just weeks before his death, Mike Voisin told me that he was hopeful about the Louisiana oyster industry's future. "Between what Mother Nature is already giving us, and what we achieve with this new method, we will probably end up producing more oysters than we have in the past," he said. "Oystermen have always known how to innovate and respond to change."

~⌐~

Few foods inspire the strong feelings that oysters do. As a child in Georgia with roots in Florida and the eastern seaboard, I watched members of my family devour them raw on the half shell and in the form of oyster dressing during Thanksgiving and Christmas dinners. I ate my fair share, but it wasn't until I moved to Louisiana that I started eating them with the kind of zeal I'd witnessed in impassioned oyster lovers. Maybe it was the company I kept. Oysters are my husband's favorite food, and we make a point of eating them frequently—both raw and cooked—when the weather finally cools and plump oysters are at their peak.

You can't beat raw on the half shell when it's oyster season, but deep-fried is an enduring way to eat oysters in Louisiana. Fried oysters, dusted lightly in cornmeal, flour, panko breadcrumbs or cracker meal, and dropped in hot oil for just a minute or two, occupy an important place on the po'boy menu, on a typical seafood platter, and on winter salads. But since the 1990s, the most popular cooked oyster recipe in Louisiana is charbroiled or char-grilled, a trend started in 1993 by Drago's Restaurant in Metairie.

It's Carnival season, the week before Mardi Gras, and I'm at Drago's to meet my friend Lee Anne Garner for an overdue visit and a couple dozen charbroiled oysters. Drago's original location sits in the Fat City neighborhood of Metairie, the New Orleans suburb, a bustling, racially diverse area that used to feature racy nightlife. Drago and Klara Cvitanovich opened their seafood restaurant here in 1969. Being part of the south Louisiana Croatian community, they sourced their oysters from Croatian-American oystermen in Plaquemines Parish. After years of serving oysters raw and fried, their son and the current manager Tommy

Cvitanovich developed a different way to prepare them. He arranged oysters on the half shell on a fiery grill and doused them with shower of garlic butter sauce. In the couple of minutes it took to cook them, he sprinkled the oysters with finely grated parmesan and Romano cheeses and dried parsley. That's about it. Since then, Drago's charbroiled oysters have become so popular that the restaurant serves about nine hundred dozen of them daily at its two locations, here and in the French Quarter.

The oysters are exceptionally tasty. Post-Katrina New Orleans is rife with a new generation of chefs whose culinary point of view is defined by restraint and ingredient integrity, but Drago's is part of the city's unapologetically indulgent culinary tradition. On each half shell, the grated cheeses have coalesced to form pieces of crust, under which the tender oysters, their edges curled, lie in flavorful sauce. Lee Anne and I pry the oysters up from their shells with our forks, pop them into our mouths, and rip pieces of flaky French bread to sop up the remaining buttery puddles. We, and everyone around us in the restaurant, seem to be eating Drago's famed oysters exclusively on this mild Friday afternoon, otherwise ignoring the vast menu. It is indeed the thing that everyone comes for. The cooks behind the grilling station in the center of the eatery are working hard to keep up with orders, and by the time we leave, the parking lot is crawling with cars. We hop in Lee Anne's Volkswagen bug and head into the Crescent City. We've planned a progressive oyster lunch and Drago's was just the first stop.

Garden District Char-grilled Oysters

A burlap sack of live oysters purchased from a seafood market is an inexpensive way of feeding a large group of oyster lovers. Bring home a sack, light the grill, plop them onto the grates and wait a minute or two for the shells to open. Smoked oysters are a crowd pleaser, and they come with an important by-product: oyster shells. One of the best moves I've made as a home cook was holding on to several dozen expended half shells following a neighborhood oyster party around our grill. After cleaning the shells thoroughly in bleach and soap and water, I've been able to store them and pull them out when I want to make Oysters Rockefeller, Oyster Bienville, or my own char-grilled oysters.

Serves 2.

> 1 stick unsalted butter, softened
> 1 large clove garlic, minced
> ½ teaspoon Worcestershire sauce
> 2 tablespoons chopped parsley
> ½ teaspoon salt
> Several grinds of fresh cracked black pepper
> A few dashes of Tabasco or Crystal hot sauce
> 1 pint Louisiana oysters
> 1 dozen, or more, clean oyster shells
> Toasted baguette, for serving

Using a fork, blend softened butter with garlic, Worcestershire sauce, parsley, salt, pepper, and hot sauce, and ease mixture onto a sheet of plastic wrap. Use wrap to help form butter into a log. Secure wrap, and place butter log in freezer for 2 hours, or long enough to make it easy to slice. Meanwhile, light coals and allow them to reach medium heat. Place one fresh raw oyster (two if they're small) onto clean oyster shells. Top each with a slice of compound butter. Grill for 2 to 3 minutes, or until oysters curl. Serve with a toasted baguette.

Fried Oysters

There is ongoing debate about how best to batter and fry oysters, but one thing is agreed, don't overcook them! If you batter them properly and your oil is hot enough, you should only need to fry the oysters for about 90 seconds to 2 minutes. Otherwise, they'll be tough and chewy. Fried oysters aren't just for po'boys or seafood platters. We also love them in delicate salads with winter lettuces and fresh herbs.

Serves 4.

    Canola oil for frying
    ¾ cup milk
    1 egg
    Hot sauce
    ¾ cup cracker meal, or ½ cup panko breadcrumbs and ¼ cup
        cornmeal combined
    ½ teaspoon salt
    ¼ black pepper
    1 pint shucked Louisiana oysters

Pour oil to a depth of 3 inches in a heavy pot and heat to medium high. While oil is heating, combine milk, egg, and a few dashes of hot sauce in a bowl and set aside. Combine cracker meal with salt and black pepper and set aside. Line a cookie sheet or large plate with wax paper. Line another with paper towels.

Remove oysters one at a time from container and inspect with your fingers for grit and shells. Dip each oyster briefly in wet batter, then roll in dry batter to coat thoroughly. Gently shake off excess, and place on cookie sheet lined with wax paper. Refrigerate until oil is heated (chilling oysters helps batter adhere).

When oil reaches 370 degrees F with a candy thermometer, it's ready. Oil is hot enough if oysters become golden brown and curl at the edges in about 1 minute. Drop in enough oysters to fit comfortably, but not crowd pan. Remove when done and place on platter with paper towels. Serve immediately.